Improving
Discussion
Leadership

IMPROVING DISCUSSION LEADERSHIP

Ronald T. Hyman
Department of Science and Humanities Education
Graduate School of Education
Rutgers University

Teachers College
Columbia University
New York   1980

Library of Congress Cataloging in Publication Data

Hyman, Ronald T.
  Improving discussion leadership.

  Includes index.
  1. Forums (Discussion and debate)   I. Title.
LC6515.H95   808.53   80-15146
ISBN 0-8077-2610-9

Designed by Julie E. Scott

9 8 7 6 5 4 3 2 1   86 85 84 83 82 81 80

Manufactured in the U.S.A.

For my parents

CONTENTS

PREFACE

This book stems from my experience as a professional and as a lay person. As a professional I have been involved in studying the verbal interaction among teachers and students in the class-room and in the conferences between supervisors and teachers held in conjunction with the observation and evaluation processes. I have also conducted discussions with students in my university classes and with colleagues and students in formal and informal settings. As a lay person I have conducted discussions with other community members to further our participation and work in civic affairs. Both as a professional and as a lay person I have been a member of many discussion groups in which I have not served as leader.

My concern for improving discussion leadership led me to read, talk, and think about the skills needed to conduct an effective, excellent discussion. I adopted some ideas I found in the literature, adapted others, and devised additional activities to help me improve my leadership ability. By reflecting on my experiences alone and with others I was able to relate my practice to my evolving concept of what a discussion is and what the skills needed for leadership are.

Along the line, I began to share my ideas with colleagues and students. What came to light was the "emperor's clothes" phenomenon. That is, for years many people have believed that discussion is a valid and beneficial approach to teaching and group thinking. Yet, virtually no one receives training in leading a discussion, a highly complex set of frequent interactions among people. Moreover, few people readily admit that they lack the training they need, primarily because, I believe, it never dawns on them that training in such a common activity is needed or even helpful. After all, just as we do not usually get training in such common and fundamental skills as listening and speaking neither do we need training in discussion leading. Only when faced with the realization that excellent discussion leading is a skill and not as simple to perform as many untrained people think, do people admit that they need some help in improving their ability to conduct a discussion.

One outgrowth of all this activity is a class at Rutgers devoted in large measure to discussion leading. (The course is entitled "Questioning and Discussion Leadership," in which I focus on the two fundamental skills of teachers and group leaders identified in the title.) I have found that the students, who are educators in a variety of roles in a variety of institutions, have been able to improve their skills right from the start by implementing the suggestions and activities that constitute this book. The comments of the students have been consistently positive as they have reflected on their improved abilities.

Improving Discussion Leadership presents the essence of my personal experience in searching for a way to improve my discussion leadership and to help others improve theirs. The book includes a self-survey of discussion leadership, which I urge you to take twice—as a way of assessing your current status and then your perceived changes—the key characteristics of a discussion, illustrative discussion excerpts, a ten-point approach to planning a discussion, a four-stage strategy for preventing and solving discussion problems, guidelines for getting and giving feedback, forms to help you specify areas needing improvement, and a mini-course in logic to help you keep a discussion on its desired goals. Central to the entire book are the two chapters presenting the six fundamental skills of discussion leading. For each skill there are guidelines for using the skill as well as suggestions for how to practice it as you progress through the book.

This is an active book in that you are invited to go beyond reading and to enter the realm of practice. To help you improve your discussion leadership is the explicit goal of this book, and, therefore, you should try out the suggestions as you go along. Be ready and free to adapt the ideas to suit your personal style.

Improvement will come as you try out new ideas and reflect on your experiences. Satisfaction will also come as you note how you have changed. Such satisfaction, the inner joy that comes from the realization of improved competence with a set of complex skills, is a reward worth striving for as you work with a group of people thinking together for mutual benefit.

Ronald T. Hyman
New Brunswick, N.J.
February 13, 1980

1

THE SELF-SURVEY OF
DISCUSSION LEADERSHIP

Before proceeding, please respond to the Self-Survey of Discussion Leadership below. When you finish, score yourself by following the instructions on the Scoring Sheet appearing after it.

It is important for you to respond to the Self-Survey so that you can know how you see yourself before reading and using this book.

Please take a few minutes to respond and score yourself. The remaining part of this chapter assumes that you have done this.

Self-Survey of Discussion Leadership

Circle the appropriate letter next to each item to indicate your response.

A = Always   O = Occasionally   N = Never
F = Frequently   S = Seldom

In a discussion group I —

A F O S N   1. accept negative behavior of individuals as everyone's problem, not just of the individuals who are disruptive.

A F O S N   2. am aware of the verbal tones I use and the messages they convey.

A F O S N   3. arrange for a physical environment that fosters positive exchanges among the discussants.

A F O S N   4. ask others about the relevancy of their remarks.

A F O S N   5. ask questions of others to elicit needed data, explanations, or opinions.

A F O S N   6. ask the discussants to draw conclusions as we end the discussion.

A F O S N   7. boast, horse around, or talk sarcastically.

A F O S N   8. change the topic and cause the group to leave its task temporarily.

A F O S N   9. check my perceptions about what's going on by asking questions such as "Am I right in saying that you feel that . . . ?"

A F O S N   10. clarify points made by others, clearing up misunderstandings, definitions, or explanations.

A F O S N   11. consider leadership of the discussion as the responsibility of everyone.

A F O S N   12. contribute to the formulation of the group's goals and procedures.

A F O S N   13. dominate the discussion.

A F O S N   14. encourage and allow the discussion questions to be answered by all the discussants, especially the quiet and shy ones.

A F O S N   15. focus the discussion at various points so that the group knows what the specific topic is and does not drift.

A F O S N   16. force quiet discussants to participate.

A F O S N   17. interfere with the group's task by arguing,

bringing up "dead issues," or persistently pleading a special interest position.

A F O S N 18. interrupt other speakers to say what's on my mind and relevant at the moment.

A F O S N 19. keep track of time and keep the discussion on schedule.

A F O S N 20. let others know when I've modified a position I took earlier.

A F O S N 21. listen attentively to others.

A F O S N 22. listen only to experts on the topic under discussion.

A F O S N 23. offer compromises when the group is deadlocked during a controversial issue.

A F O S N 24. offer needed facts and explanations to help the discussion.

A F O S N 25. praise others when they make pertinent remarks.

A F O S N 26. prepare a concise introduction of the topic to make it clear what we're discussing.

A F O S N 27. prepare a discussion strategy based on the major questions that need to be answered.

A F O S N 28. prepare an outline of the topic with suggested time limits for each phase of the discussion.

A F O S N 29. probe others for further points for clarification.

A F O S N 30. propose future activities as follow-ups to the discussion.

A F O S N 31. offer my opinions and justifications to help the discussion.

A F O S N 32. provide for a written record of the high points of the discussion.

A F O S N 33. raise the question of how the group should proceed in conducting the discussion.

A F O S N 34. reflect back to the group the verbal and non-verbal messages I receive from other discussants.

A F O S N   35. speak briefly so that others have the opportunity to talk.

A F O S N   36. state the essence of the discussion at various points as we proceed.

A F O S N   37. suggest alternative ways to view a point already raised.

A F O S N   38. suggest special discussion roles for various people as a way of involving and supporting them.

A F O S N   39. suggest ways to solve problems that have arisen because of tension and conflict in the group.

A F O S N   40. suggest when and how the group can deal with peripheral issues not taken up at the moment.

A F O S N   41. support the right of others to speak, especially those with unpopular points of view.

A F O S N   42. take steps, even before the discussion begins, to break up potentially harmful cliques.

A F O S N   43. threaten others with the pointed questions I ask and the tone in which I ask them.

A F O S N   44. try to prevent problems and a negative climate from arising.

A F O S N   45. try to reduce tension with humor or friendly comments so as to reconcile disagreements among people.

A F O S N   46. use analogies to help clarify the meaning of what has been said.

A F O S N   47. use guests as speakers and resource people.

A F O S N   48. use my physical location and posture to convey a positive nonverbal message.

A F O S N   49. view discussion as a game with winners and losers.

A F O S N   50. withdraw from the discussion and show signs of being noninvolved or indifferent.

COMMENTARY AND EXPLANATION

As you probably figured out while responding to the Self-Survey of Discussion Leadership, it is not a random collection of items relating to discussion leadership. Rather, it contains fifty items that flow from a particular viewpoint about groups and discussions. There is no secret that the underpinning of the Self-Survey, as shown by the items themselves and by their scoring, presents a position about discussion leadership. The chapters of this book will explain this position.

A clarification of three possible positions you as leader can take in discussion groups is in order. First, there is the *leader-centered group*, in which you are the focal point, making decisions for the group with your power and status in mind. You derive power from the group and at the same time give your good name, direction, and motivation to the group. You are the hub of the group, and the group fails to function effectively without you. You choose the topic and focus the discussion along lines that further personal ideas and commitments. You set the tone of the discussion by the ideas you raise and by the manner in which you raise them.

Second, there is the *leader-guided group*, in which you have a strong commitment to the progress of the group. You may be selected by the group explicitly or may emerge from the group as leader since you are looked up to for guidance in directing the flow of ideas. In either case, you are not concerned with personal power or status. You function so that the group can accomplish its purpose. You may suggest a topic to the group for approval or take the topic suggested by the group decision. You focus the discussion and serve as guide or facilitator so that members can participate to their fullest.

In the interest of the group, you function as a leader by contributing facts and opinions, clarifying ideas, reflecting back messages received, and raising procedural questions. First and foremost, you think of the group and, therefore, prefer other members to perform as best they can by sharing responsibility

Scoring Sheet for Self-Survey of Discussion Leadership

Write your score next to the number for each item in the self-survey.

For Columns I, II, III, and IV

Always = A = 4
Frequently = F = 3
Occasionally = O = 2
Seldom = S = 1
Never = N = 0

For Column V

Never = N = 4
Seldom = S = 3
Occasionally = O = 2
Frequently = F = 1
Always = A = 0

I	II	III	IV	V
1 ____	14 ____	28 ____	38 ____	7 ____
2 ____	15 ____	29 ____	39 ____	8 ____
3 ____	19 ____	30 ____	40 ____	13 ____
4 ____	20 ____	31 ____	41 ____	16 ____

5 ____	21 ____	32 ____	42 ____	17 ____
6 ____	23 ____	33 ____	44 ____	18 ____
9 ____	24 ____	34 ____	45 ____	22 ____
10 ____	25 ____	35 ____	46 ____	43 ____
11 ____	26 ____	36 ____	47 ____	49 ____
12 ____	27 ____	37 ____	48 ____	50 ____
Total ____	Total ____	Total ____	Total ____	Total ____

Total Column I ____
Total Column II ____
Total Column III ____
Total Column IV ____
Total Column V ____

Put your total Discussion Leadership Score here: [ ]   The maximum is 200 points.

for leading the group. You are concerned with fostering each member's and the group's growth rather than with seeking your own accomplishment.

Third, there is the *group-centered group*, in which there is no official leader, nor has any single member emerged to deserve the label of leader. All members hold the responsibility for leadership, performing leadership functions as they are able at different times. At any given point in time one person may appear to be *the* leader, but, in reality, all members function as leaders. It is just that for a short given time one member takes a more noticeable position than others due to self-selection or recognition by the others that this person has expertise in a particular area. No one person in particular focuses the discussion, gives feedback, or cares for the physical environment, since it is the responsibility of everyone to do so.

With these three types of discussion groups in mind, it is possible for you to better understand the framework for the Self-Survey of Discussion Leadership. The self-survey is designed around the belief that the first type of group, the leader-centered group, is not the desired type of discussion group. In fact, a leader-centered group may have a difficult, if not an impossible, time conducting a discussion if we conceive of a discussion as an open interchange among participants for the establishment of a conclusion on a given topic. (See Chapter 2 for a full examination of what a discussion is.) Rather, the collection of fifty items in the self-survey and the scoring of it support the belief that a leader-guided group or a group-centered group is the preferred type of discussion group. In both of these types each member shares responsibility for the positive functioning of the group. It is for this reason that items in column V in the scoring sheet such as changing the topic, dominating the discussion, and withdrawing are considered negative behaviors.

Both of these types, leader-guided group and group-centered group, are preferred because the focal point for decisions is the benefit of the discussion group itself. Neither is necessarily always better than the other, for each has its appropriate place. It is certainly true that mature people need to become self-generating, self-motivating, and self-directing, and thus act without a leader. Yet, at times, even with mature discussants, but especially with younger people, a leader-guided group is necessary for the effective functioning of the group due to expertise, experience, lack of knowledge about each other, size of the group, and age of the discussants. The same is true of a classroom situation or other formal situations where an official leader of the group already exists.

With this preference for shared leadership and the benefit of the group itself, it is easy to understand why such items as checking perceptions about what's going on (#9), supporting the right of others to speak (#41), and accepting negative behavior of an individual as everyone's problem (#1) are considered positive items. Equally understandable is the position that boasting, horsing around, or talking sarcastically (#7), interrupting other speakers (#18), and viewing the discussion as a game of winners and losers (#49) are negative items that those who share leadership should try to avoid.

In short, the forty positive items and the ten negative items of the self-survey stem from a definite position about discussion groups. They represent a point of view based on experience and a theoretical commitment to the benefit of rational group interaction. More than that they serve as a brief summary of desirable and undesirable leadership behaviors. Hence, they can serve as a guide for your future leadership in a discussion group and a means of assessing your position regarding group discussion for the benefit of the group.

Because some items in the self-survey are negative (column V) while some are positive (columns I, II, III, and IV), it is necessary to reverse the scoring in order to compensate for the ten negative items. Thus, Always counts 4 points for the positive items since these are desirable group leadership behaviors, whereas it yields no points for the negative items since these are behaviors to avoid. Similarly, the point values for Frequently, Seldom, and Never also switch when going from the positive to the negative items. Therefore, with this system, as shown on the scoring sheet, the maximum possible points for the self-survey is 200.

The interpretation of your discussion leadership score is easy to determine—the higher your score the closer you are to the preferred leadership behavior of a leader-guided group or group-centered group. If your score is 100 or better, then you already lean toward the preferred leadership behavior. But whatever your score, your goal should be to improve your leadership behavior, and you can do this by reading the chapters that follow and practicing the skills presented in them. You can measure your improvement at any time by checking back to the self-survey. When you finish going through the book, you can then take the same self-survey at the end of Chapter 8. You will thus be able to evaluate the difference between the two scores.

2

WHAT IS A DISCUSSION?

A DISCUSSION IS FIRST AND FOREMOST A SOCIAL ACTIVITY. Though a person on stage in a large hall such as a professor, a preacher, or a candidate for political office may say, "Today I shall discuss the importance of peace to those of us gathered here," by no means do we in the audience participate in a discussion. We may hear a lecture or a sermon or a campaign speech, but we do not fool ourselves into believing that *we discussed* the topic for that day. *We listened*, and the *speaker spoke*. So, what is a discussion?

Each discussion is different from every other one and at the same time similar to every other one. Each shares with the others the same seven key *characteristics*, the same three *realms*, and the same three *phases*. There are different *types* of discussion, five treated in this book, but, within each type, discussions follow a common strategy. Let us look at these four dimensions of every discussion as an answer to the question, What is a discussion?

Many people use the term "discussion" loosely because there are no universally set rules for answering in absolute terms any of the following questions:

1. How long must or should a discussion last?

2. What is the maximum number of people that should be in a discussion group?
3. What is the optimum number of people for a discussion group?
4. What is the best topic to discuss?
5. Who should lead the discussion?
6. What is the most amount of time a given discussant should talk during a discussion?
7. When is the optimal time for a discussion to take place?
8. Where is the best place to hold a discussion?
9. What is the best way to evaluate a discussion to determine its success?
10. What is the maximum number of discussions you should lead with the same group?

The lack of absolute answers to these ten questions—and at least a score more that you could generate in a short while—is not the reason for using discussion in a broad sense. Rather, people use the term discussion to apply to many activities because they wish to cast those activities in a good light. Discussion is an activity we all are favorably inclined to support in our Western democratic society because of the participation involved with it. And we are willing to participate in a discussion because of the positive qualities of equality, order, and reason that a discussion has. Hence, the professor, preacher, and political candidate say, "Today, I shall discuss" as an attempt to induce their audiences to transfer to their activities the virtues of a discussion. They want the audience to approve of what they are doing because the activity is a discussion, and a discussion is a worthwhile endeavor.

Perhaps this reason is wrong or only partially correct. Perhaps there are other reasons for applying the term discussion to many other activities. In any case, it remains true that a discussion *is not* a lecture, nor a sermon, nor a campaign speech, nor a debate, nor a conversation, nor an argument. It *is* something unique; it is something whose key elements need to be identified so you can have a clearer idea about what you are learning to do when you learn to lead a discussion—which is the purpose of this book.

ESSENTIAL CHARACTERISTICS OF A DISCUSSION

The following are seven essential characteristics of a discussion, as the term is used here. No attempt is made to define precisely what a discussion is, but an attempt is made to offer a set of elements to guide you in thinking about a discussion. If you wish, you may consider that these elements constitute a working definition so as to foster clear communication. Let us begin by repeating the key characteristic mentioned in the very first sentence of this chapter.

Social Activity

A person alone cannot discuss a topic such as "Alternatives to Nuclear Energy" or "Should the United Nations Dissolve Itself?" Discussion requires several people to orally exchange ideas. Since a discussion benefits when people react to each other, a discussion requires as a minimum a small group of people exchanging ideas with each other. Two people can react to each other, but the pool of human resources is too small with just one person listening and then reacting to the speaker. The minimum size for a small group discussion is five, since with two, three, or four members each person is required to be too prominent, causing a strain in the group. With five members there is still great opportunity to talk, and yet members have the benefit of being able to shift roles within the group. With five members the group gains the advantages of a complex set of interactions due to a sizable pool of human resources and the group still has little strain due to the small number of discussants.*

Cooperative Endeavor

Cooperation distinguishes the discussion from an argument and a debate that thrive on competition. In a discussion the participants enter with the notion that they will help each other study the problem before them. In contrast to a debate where

---

*A. P. Hare, *Handbook of Small Group Research*, 2nd ed. (New York: The Free Press, 1976), pp. 229-31.

cooperation is limited to an agreement to abide by the rules of the debate format, there is no winner and loser in a discussion. If the problem isn't solved or the topic not thoroughly explored, the entire group loses and there is no winner. If the group succeeds in solving the problem presented, then everyone is a winner. Social cooperation therefore requires of the discussants to be flexible in approaching a topic because inflexibility turns the tone of the discussion negative—to disputing, taking sides, obstructing.

Rational and Purposeful

Reason and purpose distinguish a discussion from free conversation among friends, where people raise topics and drop them quickly as new ideas pop into their heads through association, however remote, with something said. "That reminds me about last weekend when I saw Tom. You know he's working now at Andover's . . ." is a common type of statement in conversation. With one link connecting to another the chain of conversation grows. In contrast to conversation, discussion has a focus on an agreed-upon topic. Drifting away from the topic defeats the purpose of the discussion, whether implicit or explicit, because relevance counts.

Discussion requires the participants to think reflectively—to weigh pro and con arguments, to be objective, to consider alternative ideas, to follow the rules of logic—in order to achieve their goal. "If you do this, then such and such will occur" is a typical and common form of reasoning in a discussion. If you err in your thinking, someone is likely to correct you—not to show you up but to permit the discussion to proceed as it should. It is for the good of the discussion that errors of fact or thinking are corrected because participants strive for understanding and have a sense of common purpose in achieving their goal of studying or solving a problem. "Understanding, not victory, is the object of discussion."† Reasoned talk is the method of discussion.

---

†John Passmore, *Talking Things Over*, 3rd ed. (Melbourne: Melbourne University Press, 1963), p. 2.

Systematic

The characteristic of being systematic dovetails with the previous one. Because the discussion has a purpose, there follows that there will be some order to the subtopics raised. Different people will plan and see different possible orders, since there is no absolute or mandatory way for discussiong any complex problem worthy of the discussants' time. Nevertheless, there is a progression in a discussion—even with some short detours or backtrackings to pick up loose ends—that fosters the attainment of the goal. Discussion cannot occur when there is no sense of plan or strategy, when switching from subtopic to subtopic and back again happens. Chaos is the enemy of understanding and reason.

Creative

A discussion creates its own script. As participants ask each other questions, respond to them, and react to the comments they hear, they create the discussion. This characteristic clearly separates discussion from a formal debate, a lecture, or a speech. In these activities the participants know ahead of time what they will say and prepare their remarks. Only in a small degree is there extemporaneous shifting from or embellishing of the prepared remarks chosen for transmission. Indeed, many people read their lectures or speeches while the audience wonders why they, too, couldn't read them at a time and place of their own choosing. In contrast to lecturers, participants in a discussion create an inquiry into the topic at hand *through* their cooperative rational efforts; they do not transmit predetermined remarks. It is possible to write all the remarks down afterwards, but there is no way to know ahead of time just what the script will be. Creativity at work takes unpredictable turns because it involves reactions to the ongoing process. It is for this reason that people often say "You know, I never thought I held that opinion before," as they reflect on what happened to them during a discussion.

Requires Participation

Discussion requires listening and speaking. Active, attentive listeners are necessary for a discussion as much as active, responsive speakers are. Since discussion is creative and speakers shape their remarks as they interpret the verbal and nonverbal reactions of others, attentive listeners are needed to guide speakers. Speakers and listeners are all integral participants. When someone withdraws, either not speaking or not listening, the discussion suffers. A ripple effect sets in to affect others as they speak and listen. A broad range of viewpoints from participants benefits the discussion and gives it creative power. Though withdrawal by a lecture audience member may have an effect on the lecturer, the speaker can and generally does continue as planned without modification of the prepared remarks. The effect is minimal at most. Not so in a discussion.

Involves Leadership

In order to keep a discussion focused, rational, purposeful, creative, systematic, and broadly participatory, there is a need for leadership. In most discussions there is a designated leader; in others an informal, unappointed leader often emerges. In all discussions the discussion functions best when the leadership is shared in some measure. This means that every participant bears some responsibility for keeping the group on its topic, clarifying points raised, contributing to the study of the problem, and performing other discussion skills to be treated later (see Chapters 4 and 5).

In summary, then, there are seven key characteristics of a discussion:

1. Discussion is a social activity that takes place with a group of people.
2. Discussion is a cooperative endeavor.
3. Discussion is rational and purposeful.
4. Discussion is systematic and ordered.
5. Discussion is creative.
6. Discussion requires active participation.
7. Discussion involves leadership.

These seven characteristics together make discussion unique, different in some important way from other forms of dealing with a problem individually or in a group. Because of these characteristics people hold discussion in high esteem and understandably so. Because of these characteristics people use the term "discussion" to apply to something else so we will approve of that activity as they mask what it is they are doing. Few people, if any, oppose reason, participation, creativity, purposefulness, leadership, planning, cooperation, and social participation, and these are the elements that constitute a unique positive cluster called discussion. Together these characteristics set discussion apart from lecture, speech, debate, conversation, and argument and simultaneously raise it above these others as a method for creatively studying a problem.

REALMS OF A DISCUSSION

Every discussion has three realms that you must be concerned with as a leader. They are the substantive realm, the social-emotional realm, and the procedural realm. It would help if you had three separate eyes, so to speak, so you could keep one on each realm. But since you don't, keeping yourself alert to these three realms of the discussion becomes a complex affair. Nevertheless, you can understand what's going on in toto and act appropriately once you are sensitive to these three realms and their interactions.

Substantive Realm

The substantive realm is the most obvious one. In this realm you are concerned with the topic being discussed and what the discussants are saying about it. The topic should be relevant to the discussants so that they will be willing to discuss it openly. Also, you must consider whether or not the discussion is drifting off its topic. In addition to relevance and focus, you are concerned with truth and rationality. If a discussant makes important statements about the topic that are false, you must either correct them or provide for their correction. For example, if someone says in a discussion on "Improving the Olympics" that the Russians and the Americans threatened to go to war with each other as a result of Canadian mismanagement of the 1976 Olympic Games in Montreal, then such a statement deserves your close attention for correction.

Similarly, suppose someone says, "Well, you know that the 1980 Olympics took place in Moscow and the 1976 Olympic Games were in Montreal. So it must be that they were in Moscow in 1980 to repair the political damage done during the Canadian–Soviet feud over wheat exports in the 1960s." As leader you must correct or provide for correction of this statement because it commits a logical fallacy. One event following another is not a valid reason for concluding that the first event is the cause of the second. It is quite difficult to show that one event is the cause of another, and mere time sequence surely is inadequate to establish such a causal relationship. Sometimes it is difficult to keep track of the truth and validity of statements that seem to fly by so quickly in a discussion. Nevertheless, as you listen and contribute you must concern yourself with the logical aspect of the substantive realm as well as the relevance, truth, and focus of the discussants' remarks. See the Appendix, Mini-Course in Logic for the Discussion Leader, for further help in this matter.

Social-Emotional Realm

In the social-emotional realm, you are concerned with the prevailing atmosphere. Surely, it is possible for discussants to be truthful, logical, and relevant and yet have a discussion climate so negative as to encourage some people to be silent and fearful. It is possible to have a substantively sound discussion and at the same time have one that leaves discussants angry or frustrated and with a sense of dissatisfaction.

A climate that fosters fruitful exchanges among discussants is one in which people respect each other, and one in which they are cooperative, open, warm, and trusting. They do not attack each other with anger or sarcasm. A favorable climate encourages the discussants to interact in such a way as to feel satisfied about their efforts of studying the problem at hand. A negative climate leads discussants to withdraw or react angrily to each other and thus not attain their goal of collectively studying a problem. The overall reaction in a negative atmosphere is one of dissatisfaction and frustration.

You must be concerned with this second realm. You must take steps to create and maintain a positive atmosphere. At times you will not succeed in solving a problem through group discussion. However, if you have created a favorable social-emotional climate, the discussants will most likely be willing to pursue the topic further at another time. You have not jeopardized future discussions. On the other hand, even if you solve a particular problem within a negative climate, you may have failed in the long run because of the sour taste left with the discussants. You may have won a battle but lost the war.

Procedural Realm

In the procedural realm, you are concerned with how the group moves toward studying the problem before it and the processes the group employs in its approach to the task. It may be that most groups do begin *without ever consciously* thinking about their discussion procedure and simply allow open and random exchanges. This may indeed account for the dullness of many discussions and the inability of the groups to succeed in achieving their goals. If you are concerned with procedure, then you can and must direct the group to make some *explicit* decisions about its own processes in the beginning of its discussion.

You are clearly concerned that the chosen topic for discussion is meaningful. The discussants should have a stake in the procedure they will follow. For example, if the group decides to hear a report from an expert before moving to open exchanges, then the discussants will be willing to listen to the expert and thus be silent for a while. If the group itself doesn't decide on procedure, then several negative results may occur: (1) The group will miss an opportunity to try an ordered, beneficial approach; (2) some of the discussants will become disgruntled about what's happening and will withdraw, saying, "We're going about this task the wrong way and I want no part of this"; and (3) since discussants have no stake in the procedure being used, they may have no stake in the results of the discussion.

The procedural realm is too often the forgotten realm. The assumption, which is wrong and harmful, is that it doesn't make a difference how the group proceeds in studying the problem. On the contrary, once the group is clear about how it will proceed and is satisfied that the procedure being used was chosen from several available ones as the appropriate one at that given time, the group will discuss the topic with a sense of commitment and enthusiasm.

For these reasons it is important for you to raise the question of procedure early. You might say, ''Well, we've got a pretty clear idea as to what's the topic, and now we've got to decide how we're going to proceed. I can think of three roads to use, and you might have several more. So before talking about the topic, let's take a minute or so to decide how we'll move. If we have to revise later on, we'll do so.''

It is important for the group to be able to suggest and modify procedures rather than only accept your suggestion routinely or merely select from among several of your suggestions. This gives the group the sense of being master of its own destiny and thus responsible for its own actions. This yields feelings of commitment and ''ownership'' toward the discussion, which are essential. You must, therefore, openly and explicitly offer the discussants the opportunity to recommend procedures in addition to yours (if you choose to offer some in the first place) and to modify the ones you suggest. Through modification and combination, even if the group doesn't offer any new procedural suggestions of its own, the group can achieve a sense of satisfaction in the procedural realm.

Sometimes a critical statement or incident seriously alters the plan for the discussion in regard to time or topic or procedure. (This is in contrast to minor drifts from the topic where, on your own, you direct the group along the road that it had chosen earlier.) When you arrive at a crucial juncture, then it is necessary and appropriate to halt the substantive flow of the discussion and to open the floor to suggestions on procedure so that the group can make its own decision again. You are entitled to offer possibilities for the group to consider, but, for the health of the discussion, you must not dictate to the group how it should proceed.

PHASES OF A DISCUSSION

Just as a story and a play have a beginning, a middle, and an end, so, too, does every discussion have a structure consisting of a beginning, a middle, and an end.‡ There is a difference, however, and this difference sets a discussion off from a story and a play.

Beginning Phase

The beginning phase of a discussion consists of three subparts. First comes the introduction of the topic. Here the discussants with your help as leader clarify what is the question before them. The clarification of the topic indicates what type of discussion will occur and what precisely is the question which the discussants must answer. Then the discussants decide on how they will approach the question. They decide on how to proceed so as to best utilize their resources.

The last part of the beginning phase is the making of an assertion that elicits exchanges among members. For example, suppose your group is discussing the question, "Should the United States withdraw from the United Nations?" Until someone takes a position by answering the topic question yes or no *and* also states the facts about it or gives reasons for it, the discussion cannot and does not begin. A simple yes or no answer does not suffice since that is not something that other members can consider and investigate for accuracy and reasonableness. If someone says, "Yes, the United States should withdraw because the UN has caused more wars than it has settled or prevented," then members can discuss the assertion made. Now, the discussion has rightfully begun.

Middle Phase

The middle phase of a discussion also has several subparts. What these subparts are depends on what type of discussion is occurring. The middle parts of a policy—problem solving, ex-

---

‡Ibid., pp. 12-22.

plaining, predicting, and reflective discussion—are all different, and it is this middle part which distinguishes one type from the other. For specifics on these middle parts, see Chapter 3 on planning a discussion.

End Phase

The end phase of a discussion consists of three parts. In the first part of this closing phase, the discussants reach their conclusions based on their examination (middle phase) of the assertions (beginning phase) made by the discussants. In the second part of the end phase a discussant, or more often you as leader, recapitulates the key points made during the discussion. In the final part the discussants and you suggest ideas for launching new activities based on the discussion. For specifics on performing the discussion skill of introducing and closing, see Chapter 5 on discussion skills.

In summary, then, there is a general structure to all discussions:

1. Beginning Phase
   a. Introducing and clarifying question for discussion
   b. Introducing question of procedure
   c. Making assertions on the topic
2. Middle Phase
   Examining the assertions made (the sub-parts differ depending on the type of discussion)
3. End Phase
   a. Drawing conclusions
   b. Recapitulating
   c. Launching new activities

TYPES OF DISCUSSION

No two discussions are alike. Discussions differ naturally because there are different members; they occur at different times, they have different lengths, they have different topics, and they take place in different settings. Moreover, they differ because there are different *types of discussion*, and each type by its very nature requires the discussants to travel along a different path. Thus, it is essential for you as leader to be fully aware of what type of discussion you are involved in with your group.

Policy Discussion

The policy discussion focuses on how the group should act regarding a particular issue. For example, if your group is the board of directors of the local community center, you may have policy discussions on: "Should the community center establish a branch in the new, growing section of town?" "Should the community center continue to run a summer overnight camp in light of decreasing enrollment?" "Should our local community center support the national organization in its decision to approve a senator's plan for abortion law reform?" Depending on the outcome of the discussion, the board of trustees will take actions to implement its policy decision.

Sometimes a group can have a policy discussion on an issue where it cannot act on its own decision. For example, a group of people at the local community center or students at school could discuss the question, "Should the United States withdraw from the United Nations?" Indeed, the topic qualifies as one of public policy, but the group cannot act on its decision to withdraw, if it so decides. It can continue the discussion with other people and write letters to government officials who do have the power to take action on this matter.

The essential characteristic of a policy discussion, whether or not the group can act on its decision, is the taking of a stand. If the question before the group is "Should the United States withdraw from the United Nations?," then the group together (if it desires a group decision) or each member individually must answer the question. This question requests a yes/no response because of the way it is phrased, just as a question on a local bond issue (Should Illinois issue $1 billion worth of bonds to support three new state parks?) requires a yes/no answer in the voting booth. It is inadequate to only discuss the pros and cons of withdrawing from the UN or to only understand the President's position on the question. Since it is a policy question, the discussants must take a value position on the matter once they have discussed the pros and cons and other preliminary matters.

Sometimes it is necessary to distinguish between issues that are a matter of *public* policy and those that are *not public* policy. A public policy issue is one which concerns the public because the government or some other tax-supported or government-supported group (for example, the post office, the Tennessee Valley Authority, and the Federal Reserve Board) must decide on it. If the group responsible for making the decision is not acting on behalf of the broad tax-paying public but on behalf of its members, then the policy it creates is not considered a *public policy*. This is true whether the group is a commercial group or a community service group such as the Red Cross that is supported by voluntary contributions. The group must follow the same procedure in taking a stand on every issue it is considering whether or not the issue is public policy.

Problem-Solving Discussion

In a problem-solving discussion the group seeks an answer to a problem or conflict facing it. Just as a policy discussion topic is characterized by "should" in the question, so a problem-solving topic has "how" in its question. For example, if your group is the board of trustees of the local community center, you might discuss such problems: "How can we improve our services to senior citizens?" "How can we increase our membership among young adults from 19 to 26?" "How can we raise money to rebuild our heated indoor swimming pool damaged by leaking pipes?"

Problem-solving questions imply a prior decision that the action should be taken. That is to say, in the above illustrative questions, it is already decided or assumed that the community center should provide better services to the senior citizens, should increase membership of young adults, and should raise money to build a heated indoor swimming pool. What remains is to decide on the steps for implementing those decisions, and the answers to the "how" questions constitute those steps. The discussion group must examine the facts relevant to its problem. It needs to discuss the pros and cons of the various recommended steps but *not* the pros and cons of providing better services, or increasing membership, or raising money in the first place since they are not the focus here.

The purpose of the problem-solving discussion, as with any discussion, is to benefit from many points of view in seeking a solution to a problem facing it. It doesn't matter whether the problem is one seeking correction of a bad situation, or one seeking to improve an existing situation, or one seeking the resolution of conflict between two situations or people. The purpose of the discussion is to decide on the appropriate steps to take after hearing what various people see as the probable consequences of the problem situation as well as the probable consequences of each of the steps suggested to solve the problem.

Explaining Discussion

A related type of discussion is the explaining discussion that analyzes the causes or reasons for a given situation. For example, your community center board of trustees group might discuss such topics as: "Why are we losing members in the 50-to-65-year-old group?" "Why is our image in the community an elitist one rather than an expected egalitarian one?" "Why do teen-agers not participate in our summer biking and camping program?" Just as "should" and "how" characterize policy and problem-solving discussions, the "why" in these questions characterizes the explaining discussion.

The explaining discussion generally serves as a prelude to a policy or problem-solving discussion, but it can also stand independently. The purpose of this type of discussion is to explain a given situation as illustrated above. An analysis discussion is also appropriate to explain a policy position held by someone else or by another group. For example, a group could discuss "Why does the president favor the restructuring of the Department of Labor?"

The explaining discussion does not require the group to take a stand nor to recommend steps for implementing a solution to a problem. Its purpose is to increase the members' understanding of the issue by exchanging views from many perspectives. With greater understanding the members will be prepared to take a stand or suggest solutions at a subsequent time in regard to related topics.

Predicting Discussion

Another related type of discussion, a complement to the explaining discussion, is the predicting discussion in which the members predict the probable consequences of a given situation or position. For example, your community center board of trustees might have a predicting discussion on such topics as: "What will happen to our community and our center when the government begins its urban renewal program next year?" "If we raise our membership dues to keep up with the inflationary prices we pay for heat, light, and maintenance wages, what will happen to our membership?" "What will be the likely effect of renting our facilities to other groups for weekend retreats or conventions?"

The predicting discussion seeks to examine the probable consequences of a situation—that is, the effects of it—just as an explaining discussion seeks to examine the causes of a situation. The predicting discussion is future oriented while the explaining discussion is past oriented. The purpose of the predicting discussion, as with the explaining discussion, is to increase the members' understanding. Hence, the predicting discussion also generally serves as a prelude to a policy or problem-solving discussion. As in the explaining discussion, the predicting discussion also does not require the discussants to take a stand on an issue or suggest steps for implementing a solution to a problem.

Debriefing Discussion

In the debriefing discussion, the discussants reflect on the facts and meaning of a shared activity. The group may have toured a historic or public site (for example, the Statue of Liberty or the National Gallery), seen a play in the theater, or participated in a mock political convention. To insure that the experience is educationally beneficial and to allow for sharing of information and impressions gained, it is necessary for you to conduct a discussion that leads the members to reflect on what happened to them.

A debriefing discussion begins with the members sharing the

facts about the activity and the feelings they had about it. It moves from there to an analysis of the facts and feelings the members have so that they can discover the meaning of the activity to them in terms of the statements and generalizations that can be made. As an aid to understanding the meaning of the activity, especially if the activity involves some form of role-playing, you help the discussants relate the activity to other aspects of their lives. The discussion then moves to exchanging ideas on related future activities which now seem appropriate. In short, the debriefing discussion seeks to ensure that the common activity has meaning for the members and seeks to serve as a springboard for launching future activities that can also benefit the group.

In summary, there are five main types of discussion:

1. Policy
2. Problem-solving
3. Explaining
4. Predicting
5. Debriefing

There are other, minor types, for sure, but for the purposes of this book, these five types of discussion will suffice to alert you as leader to the idea that different types of discussions require your group to travel different roads in pursuing its topics. (For suggested strategies to use with these five types of discussion, see Chapter 3.) Suffice it here to restate that as leader it is necessary for you to be aware of the types of discussion just as it is necessary to keep track of the three realms of a discussion and to be sensitive to the seven key characteristics of a discussion.

Although no two discussions are alike in specifics, every discussion is like every other because of the common dimensions of the key characteristics of a discussion, realms of a discussion, phases of a discussion, and types of discussion.

3

PLANNING A DISCUSSION

GOOD DISCUSSIONS SELDOM JUST HAPPEN; THEY DON'T JUST materialize by themselves. A good discussion most often results from careful planning and alert use of discussion skills. Recall the New York Knicks championship basketball team of 1970. As the team played and demonstrated "team defense" and team offense based on finding the "open man" who would have the best opportunity to score a basket, basketball looked like a simple and easy game. Other professional, collegiate, and high school teams began to copy the Knicks' style of basketball. Many, however, could not duplicate what they saw the Knicks do. Then they realized that the Knicks' style was deceptive—what looked simple and easy was a result of much planning and practice. And most teams were just not ready to plan and practice as the Knicks did. The key to cooperative success, as a basketball team or discussion group knows, is no secret—it's *planning and practicing.*

ESSENTIAL PLANNING ELEMENTS

The essential elements needed in planning are knowledge of—

1. the topic under discussion (in-depth knowledge is preferable

but not absolutely necessary; broad, survey-type knowledge is a minimum requirement);
2. the strategies appropriate to the various types of discussion;
3. and ability to perform the six discussion skills (see Chapters 4 and 5);
4. discussants who will participate;
5. the time and space conditions of the meeting room;
6. the physical and human resources available for the group's use during the discussion.

APPROACHES TO PLANNING A DISCUSSION

Let us now go into detail in regard to these elements and present a ten-point planning approach.

Choosing the Discussion Topic

Ideally you should not choose the topic. It is much better for the group to select its own topic. Relevance to the group is automatically insured when the group chooses the topic, for it signifies ownership, willingness, and interest. If the discussants don't care about the topic, they will not discuss it in a way that is meaningful to them and pleasant to you. People find it difficult, if not virtually impossible, to discuss a topic they have little or no interest in. If they don't care about the issue, they will not bother to take a stand on it, explain its causes, or predict its consequences. They will not open themselves up to share their thoughts with others if they feel that the topic is irrelevant or nonrelevant to their present needs and interests.

Sometimes, but especially if you are a teacher, you will have the task of choosing the topic. If so, you must select it in such a way that the topic grows out of the discussants' interests and needs. You must infer what they would probably choose given the current situation. If you impose a topic the group is not interested in, the discussion exchanges among members will be stilted, inhibited, or a sign of just plain lip service. Though you may believe that the group *needs* to discuss a given topic and at times the need of the group is the chief criterion for selecting a topic, need alone will not suffice.

In short, if you must choose on behalf of the group, use relevance *and* need as your criteria. Let the topic emerge as a natural one for the discussants. Just because some students are in a political science class, it does not mean that they want to or will meaningfully discuss the United States withdrawal from the United Nations. The group may be much more interested in a related topic, such as "The utopian government for one world in the 20th century: What will it be like?" Most important, you must satisfy yourself (and others, too, if you can check with them) that the question is relevant to the prospective discussants.

Phrasing the Discussion Question

Once you have a topic or issue, you need to be careful how you phrase the question to the group. Rather than choose a type of discussion and then phrase a question to fit the type, let the type of discussion flow from the question. Concern yourself with the question and not the type unless there is some special reason for doing so.

Ask yourself, "What is the central question each discussant must answer?" Then write—yes, write—it out with your own hand. Writing it out yourself is an excellent way for you to see if you have a clear and concise way of grasping the issue. Rewrite the question if it is necessary until you are satisfied that you and the other discussants will be clear about what the topic is. If you can, try out the question on someone who can provide you with a comment on the clarity of your question.

In addition to clarity, you must check on several other characteristics of the question. Be sure that the question is precise, understandable, and short. Also, except for a discussion question that seeks a value decision (for example, Should we prohibit abortions?), no question should be phrased in a yes/no format. Try to use "Why," "How," and "What" in your question. Spend time thinking about and phrasing the question. The precious time spent on "playing" with the question is an investment in the future. The old saw that a question well put is half the answer applies to discussions. The well-put question will propel you into your next two tasks: (1) examining which potentially important aspects of the issue may arise and (2) determining what type of discussion you will be leading. There is no doubt that a clear, precise, short, relevant, and understandable question is essential for success in further planning and subsequent discussing.

Outlining the Topic

Once you have an acceptable written question, start writing out the aspects of the question which you feel are important and which the discussants will likely raise. As you note the aspects of the topic, you should also note significant facts you know or need to learn before the discussion begins. For example, suppose your question is, "Should the United States withdraw from the United Nations?" You may note such aspects as financial participation, legislative participation, participation in various UN agencies (for example, UNESCO and UNICEF), and support of U.S. membership by American citizens and officials. You probably will need to check out such facts as the amount of money the United States contributed to the UN in the past few years and the way the United States voted on key matters in the UN Assembly and Security Council. In short, brush up on the UN.

You do not need to be a United Nations expert. You do need to feel confident that you have a broad understanding of the UN and the role of the United States in the United Nations. You should not feel that you ought to be or even will be the sole source of knowledge about the UN at the discussion. Other people present will know something about the UN and be able to contribute to the discussion. However, if after some study on the United Nations you still feel inadequate in terms of knowledge or if you feel that because of the significance of the topic or the needs of the group expert in-depth knowledge is needed, then plan to have an authority on the topic present along with several reference books. That UN authority will serve as your resource person during the discussion to answer pertinent questions, expand on points made by the discussants, and correct factual errors.

At this point begin outlining the issue in some order that makes sense to you. If you have asked an expert to be your resource person, ask for comments on, and suggested changes for, your outline. There is no one absolutely correct order for examining the many aspects of any complex issue—and issues you will discuss generally turn out to be complex. Therefore, as long as you have organized your issue in some rational order according to your understanding, you will have a workable outline.

Planning Your Discussion Strategy: the Beginning Phase

With your question and notes before you, determine what type of discussion you will conduct—policy, problem-solving, explaining, predicting, or debriefing. (See Chapter 2.) With this determination and further consultation with your notes, you can begin to plan your discussion strategy. At the end of this chapter there are five sample questioning strategies for your use, one for each of the five major discussion types.*

Remember that there are common elements in every discussion regarding the structure of the discussion. There is a beginning phase, a middle phase, and an end phase. Let us treat these phases and their subparts as an approach to planning your strategy.

Recall that there are three parts to the beginning phase of a discussion: introducing the topic, raising the procedural question, and making an assertion.

Introducing the Topic. When you plan your beginning phase, it is wise first to briefly read the material on the skill of introducing as offered in depth in Chapter 5. If you are at all nervous or inexperienced, it is helpful to write out your brief introduction of the topic so that you won't be long-winded, imprecise or vague.

---

*Ronald T. Hyman, *Strategic Questioning* (Englewood Cliffs, N.J.: Prentice-Hall, 1979), chapter 5.

It is vitally important to start the discussion out on the right foot and to have a clear, planned introduction so that the discussants would not be confused by a vague or incorrect statement of the issue as decided upon earlier. If you have a resource person or special audiovisual aid such as a film or tape recording, here is where you should announce your resource. Plan what you will say about the resource. Keep it *brief*.

You have two basic options now in regard to strategy. In your first option, after introducing the topic, you immediately raise the question of procedure. If you do so, you have the advantage of getting procedures out of the way so you devote all remaining time to substantive matters without a break in continuity. However, the disadvantage is that the group and you may not have enough of a grasp of the situation to determine what procedure is appropriate.

In your second basic option, after introducing the discussion question (especially in policy, explaining, or predicting discussions), you elicit several initial responses. With these responses to the discussion question on the floor, you now shift to the procedural question. For example, if in a policy discussion everyone initially responds that the United States should withdraw from the United Nations, then you may suggest proceeding with a role-playing exercise in order to bring out the negative point of view. If, however, you have a balance among the group in regard to withdrawal and continued membership in the UN, you may wish to suggest proceeding by having the pro group and then the con group submit their reasons.

The advantage of this second option is the quick diagnosis you can make of the situation. With this approach, procedure follows content. Your tailor-made suggestions for procedure can be chosen from the possibilities you have prepared. The disadvantage with this option is the break in continuity. Sometimes it is difficult for discussants who are eager to discuss an issue to halt their substantive comments for a while and shift to procedural matters. Their discussion appetite has been whetted and now they find it hard to shift from substantive matters to procedural matters and back again to substantive matters.

Thus, in anticipation of what you expect from the discussants, you should decide on your next move after introducing the substantive question—either to move directly to procedure or to elicit brief initial responses before moving to procedure. Your choice depends on your knowledge of the discussants. Either approach is correct; each works; each has its merits; and it's up to you to decide on one or the other given the situation as you assess it.

Raising the Procedural Question. After you have planned what you will do about general procedure, list some specific suggestions for consideration by the group on how to proceed discussing the question as posed. Below is a list of seven possible ways to proceed that you can modify to fit your specific group.

1. Open the floor for general responses to the question. Let the flow take it from there.
2. Ask a resource person to make an opening remark to be followed by reaction from the discussants.
3. Ask two different people with known different responses to the question to speak first and then open the floor to general exchanges.
4. Ask each person to respond to the question in moderate depth before permitting exchanges among discussants.
5. Ask one person to make a prepared statement. Follow this with a time period set aside *only* for clarification questions from the other discussants. (For example, would you please clarify your claim about the UN promoting conflict?) Follow this with a time period for exchanges of agreement and disagreement among all discussants.
6. Ask each person to make an initial response to the discussion question. Following this, show a film, play, or tape recording and have discussants react to the film or tape recording from their specific vantage point. Then have exchanges among discussants based on what they have heard.
7. Ask for initial responses. If there is no balance or even a split of differing viewpoints, have a role-playing session to bring out other viewpoints. If there is a balance or split, divide the group into subgroups. Ask each group to prepare a positional

statement and a set of questions to ask the others. Follow this with a general period of exchanges among discussants.

Write down at least three possibilities for procedure and rank them in order of your preference of what you feel would be the best way to proceed. Refer to these when you raise the question of procedure, and offer your own suggestions to the group. Remember that when you raise the procedural question you can offer suggestions and even your preferences if you wish, but you must also solicit procedural suggestions from the discussants. The group will subsequently decide on a procedure based on their own and your suggestions. They may choose not to offer any suggestions of their own, so you must be prepared with at least three for them to consider.

Eliciting an Assertion. Plan a question or some other procedure, such as a prepared statement or written report, that will elicit an assertion. Without an assertion on the floor there can be no discussion. It is the assertion—facts, reasons, advantages and disadvantages, comparisons and contrasts—which is what the discussants will exchange ideas about. In short, ask yourself and provide an answer to the question, "How will I elicit an assertion or assertions to serve as the basis of the discussion?"

Planning Your Discussion Strategy: the Middle Phase

To plan the middle phase of your discussion it is best to prepare a set of central questions which you believe need to be answered. This set of questions will consist only of the *big* or *key* questions and will not list all of the questions you and other discussants will ask during the discussion. Your task will be to see that these questions are answered as the discussants exchange ideas, whether or not you or someone else specifically asks them. *You* do not have to ask them all, but all of them should be raised.

The five basic sets of questions for the five types of discussion at the end of this chapter should serve as springboards for *you to modify* so that your set is specific to your topic and group. Note that there is a strategy to these questions in that the questions are in a particular order to provide an orderly answer to the discussion question.

Planning Your Discussion Strategy: the End Phase

Recall here that all discussion end phases share in common three important parts: drawing conclusions, recapitulating, and launching new activities. It is important, therefore, that you leave adequate time for the end phase. A discussion without a proper ending leaves the discussants dissatisfied and unsure of what they have gained from their efforts. If you must, cut the middle part short so as to have enough time for the end phase.

Drawing Conclusions. Your strategy must include a question requesting the discussants to draw a conclusion based on the many points raised. In each of the sample questioning strategies presented for the five types of discussion, there is a concluding question. As before, you need not ask it if someone steps forward to state the conclusion or if you have prearranged for someone to do this. (See page 00 on planning roles for the discussants.) In any case, it is preferable for the discussants to draw the conclusions. It is their discussion, and they should draw their own conclusions if possible. If they don't or can't draw the conclusions, then you must do so.

Recapitulating. Following the drawing of conclusions someone must recapitulate the main points of the discussion. Once again you should consult the section in Chapter 5 dealing in depth with performing the closing skill. You yourself can recapitulate the discussion or you can request someone else to do it. Your discussion needs a "recap" like a car needs a steering wheel because, depending on the recapitulation of the entire discussion, you will launch new activities based on what the discussants have accomplished.

Launching. To plan for the launching part of the end phase, if you yourself are going to perform the role, you should think of at least two possible activities to suggest to the group. These activities—trips, readings, films, further discussions, or whatever—should be projected outgrowths that probably will interest the group. As you proceed in the discussion, be alert to other suggestions and note them for mentioning later.

Remember that just as you should request suggestions from the group on how to proceed in your introduction, so, too, must you ask for suggestions regarding future activities during your closing. The group can modify or accept your suggestions, or they can accept their own. In any case, you should close with a launching for the future to give a feeling of moving forward. Keep in mind that it is no accident that for a similar reason the final activity in completing high school or college is called "Commencement."

Deciding on Your Own Role during the Discussion

In planning the discussion you must deal with yourself just as you deal with the topic, the strategy, and the discussants. It is necessary to keep your own discussion skills honed and ready for use. Review the six discussion skills presented in Chapters 4 and 5, which indicate what you can and should be doing as leader. If you need to practice performing these skills of contributing, crystallizing, focusing, introducing/closing, questioning, and supporting, then take time to practice them so that you will be sharp and ready when you lead your discussion. Every good musician and athlete practices before show time or game time. Why not you as discussion leader?

The key skill to plan for is contributing. You must carefully decide how you will contribute to the discussion. Will you be the group's own authoritative resource person? Will you present descriptions of events, comparisons, and explanations? Will you choose a film or recording to be used? It is only too easy for you to dominate the discussion by lengthy contributions wherein you give facts, explanations, and opinions. You should plan for restraint on your part in regard to contributing by arranging for the discussants to maximize their contributions.

The general rule of thumb for good leadership is to share your leadership with the discussants in regard to performing the six discussion skills and the ten discussion roles as listed in the next section. The less you explicitly do yourself and the more you provide for others to do so that what needs to be done gets done, the better. Reserve for yourself what others cannot or will not do. At the same time, you must be prepared to do everything and anything at the last minute if someone fails to perform for you.

Planning for Maximum Involvement

Sometimes every discussant will participate without any special urging or encouragement on your part. Most of the time, however, this doesn't occur, and as the group gets larger, spontaneous volunteer participation goes down. Some quiet and reserved members may feel uncomfortable performing certain roles without your special encouragement. If they do not participate, the quality of the discussion suffers.

Assigning Roles to the Discussants. To maximize involvement and to improve the quality of the discussion, it is important for you to request various discussants to perform special roles. Decide on who should do what based on your knowledge of the discussants, the type of discussion, and what will be your own role. Below is a brief list of ten roles you can use and modify to help you improve the discussion:

1. Presenter of position paper that will serve as basis for the discussion
2. Periodic summarizer (to summarize the main substantive points two to four times during the discussion)
3. Greeter and seater (to assure a positive climate and nonverbal support for various discussants)
4. Recorder (to serve as group memory)
5. Timekeeper (to keep you on schedule)
6. Designated first speaker (to break the ice after a film or recording or presentation)
7. Resource person (to serve as the expert on the specific issue)

8. End-of-discussion recapitulator
9. Launcher of future activities (to suggest new directions at the closing of the discussion)
10. Logician

Determine which of these roles you will need for your discussion. You will not need all of them for every discussion. Decide on whom you will request to perform these roles. Speak with these persons ahead of time to get their agreement and explain how you expect them to perform. For example, if you choose to have someone be periodic summarizer, you may wish to call upon that person every time you shift to another new major point in your outline. Or, you can ask the periodic summarizer to use good judgment and summarize whenever it seems necessary, usually two to four times. If you request someone to serve as timekeeper, try to decide on a schedule together based on your outline. Arrange for the timekeeper to keep you posted in some unobtrusive way so you can move ahead without disturbing the flow of the discussion.

People with special roles behave in special ways. You can use this approach of assigning roles to encourage certain people to participate more while at the same time getting others to be verbally less active. For example, if Joe Smith has dominated previous discussions, you may be able to remove him from "center stage" by asking him to serve strictly as summarizer three times during the discussion. Emphasize the importance of careful listening and astute summarizing as a contribution to the upgrading of the discussion. On the other hand, if Joe Smith has been relatively shy and quiet, speaking only once every discussion, he will find it easy to increase his participation to three times by being summarizer since it is expected of him.

Involving Discussants. You can also involve certain discussants by including them in your suggestions on procedure at the beginning of the discussion. For example, you can suggest someone in particular who has been quiet to be one of two people to offer initial responses to the discussion question. Or, you can include that same person as the focal point for one of your suggested future activities when you close the discussion. With a little planning you will be able to think of something special for the person who needs your support.

Planning Use of Time and Space

Everyone lives with time and space constraints. The discussion offers you no release from these constraints, so you might as well accept them and plan for them.

Time. There is no such thing as "there was no time to draw conclusions since we only had one-half hour to hold our discussion." If, for example, you have only thirty minutes for your total time, then allocate your time carefully to include all phases of the discussion. Take just a minute or so (no more) for your introduction of the topic and the raising of the procedural question in your beginning phase. Take another minute to elicit an assertion or two so as to begin the exchange of ideas among the discussants. Leave three minutes for your end phase to draw conclusions and close the discussion. Watch your time closely yourself and arrange for someone to perform the role of time-keeper to help you maintain a schedule. The remaining twenty-four minutes or so (80% percent of the time) is left for your middle phase. And that's time enough for worthwhile exchanges.

The point is simple—there is time provided you realize what is needed within the structure and nature of the discussion. You can allocate time for a solid beginning phase, middle phase, and end phase, as well as time for having certain members perform special roles, if you plan carefully.

Take your outline and set of strategic questions and examine them together. Write out *for yourself* in the left margin of each paper the approximate time you will allot to each phase of the discussion. Below is an illustrative annotated agenda/strategy of questions.

SAMPLE: "How Can We Improve the Olympic Games?"

Oct. 16, 9:00–9:45

9:00–9:01   1. Introduce topic of Olympics and our question above

9:01–9:04	2.	Dan to give three-minute prepared talk on Olympics, giving his personal recommendations
9:04–9:05	3.	Decide on procedural issue (see notes)
9:05–9:10	4.	What do you see as the problems facing the Olympics today in light of Dan's remarks? (Comments on Dan's remarks)
9:10–9:15	5.	What do we know about the Olympics and the sports world today that will help us in recommending improvements?
	6.	What suggested improvements do you have?
9:15–9:36	7.	What's your support—what makes you think your recommendations will actually improve the Olympics?
9:36–9:41	8.	If the Olympic Committee implemented your recommendations, what else might occur?
9:41–9:43	9.	Based on all these points, what do you conclude are the best recommendations to make to improve the Olympics?
9:43–9:45	10.	Close the discussion.
9:43–9:44		a. Recapitulate (—by Chris)
9:44–9:45		b. Launch future plans (—see notes—already have another meeting scheduled for Oct. 23.)

If you examine the above agenda/strategy, you will see that there is time allocated for each of the three phases of the discussion. Furthermore, the middle phase section most directly concerned with the discussion question has received the bulk of the time. This gives a sense of having enough time to deal with the topic adequately, given the time constraint of only forty-five minutes for the total time.

Space. Space is similar to time in that seldom do you have ideal space conditions. Sometimes the room is too small and sometimes it's too big. Whatever the space available, you have no choice but to cope with it.

Visit the discussion room if you are not familiar with it at least ten minutes ahead of time. Decide on how you want to place the furniture, especially the chairs for the discussants. Try to arrange the chairs so that everyone can easily have eye contact with everyone else. This constitutes the first general rule of space utilization. Try to arrange the chairs in the shape of an open horseshoe with a chair for yourself in the open part. This is particularly important if the group has eight or more members including yourself. This arrangement provides a better focus for you as leader than a circle, since in a circle formation the people on your immediate left and right have trouble making eye contact with you. If your group is small (5 to 7 members), a circle arrangement is fine.

GROUP SIZE: 8 or more   GROUP SIZE: 7 or less

Try to position a chalkboard or standing easel pad near you so that you can have some means of writing down significant points for the entire group to see.

The second general rule in regard to space is to keep the room arrangement flexible. You may have to shift the seating arrangement as you go along due to procedural decisions that the group will make in light of their progress. If you keep an open mind and a flexible arrangement, then you will be able to use your space wisely.

Planning Use of Physical and Human Resources

The use of a discussion aid such as a film, tape recording, or magazine article does not reflect negatively on your abilities as a discussion leader. On the contrary, when you use such resources, you gain. The quality of the discussion improves and the result is reflected positively. Just as a trumpeter in a band uses different aids to insert into the bell of the trumpet in order to get the proper sound effects, so should you use what is available to help spur exchanges among the discussants.

It is often helpful to have the discussants build on a common resource in a policy, problem-solving, explaining, predicting, or debriefing discussion. It is easy for discussants to analyze what someone else says and proposes. It is helpful if the discussants can continually refer back to something they share in common that is concrete, something that is more than words they've heard and can no longer retrieve. For these reasons you should seek out appropriate and *brief* audiovisual aids.

Possible audiovisual aids:

1. film
2. video tape recording
3. audio tape recording
4. magazine article
5. map
6. data chart
7. simulation game
8. role-playing exercise with prepared roles

Along with these resources, which capture the human mind for us via our advanced technology, you should try to make use of live guests to serve as presenters and resource people. A guest expert provides a spark, a sense of relevance, and a tone of authoritativeness that help the discussants connect the question to situations outside the discussion room.

Naturally, you should consult with your guest about the role you wish him or her to perform. Go over your time schedule, your outline, and indicate any of the roles you have asked discussants to perform. If your group wishes your guest to speak for ten minutes before open exchanges begin, then indicate this clearly. Set up a means for you to alert the speaker that time is running out—a two-minute warning, for example. Do not hesitate to stop a speaker who forgets the schedule, for it is your job to lead a discussion and not to support a lecture.

If your group wishes to use your guest as a resource person, then decide with the group during the procedural part of the beginning phase precisely what your guest's role will be. For example, the resource person could listen for ten minutes and then comment. Or, the resource person could simply respond to the members' questions so as to provide relevant data on the discussion question.

No matter how your group uses your guests, there is absolutely no need for you to feel that you are in competition with them. Guests are an aid to you and your group; they will function well when you are clear about their roles and your role as well. By planning and consulting with your guests ahead of time, you can easily reap the benefits of having guests participate in your discussion.

Even if you have a group of five people, but especially if the group is more than ten, try to have a chalkboard or large easel pad available for writing down important points. Each of these provides the necessary means for keeping public what has been said, keeping points and decisions available for easy reference, and focusing the attention of the group on a given point.

The large easel pad on a stand, though smaller than a chalkboard and perhaps a bit harder to write on, is preferable because you can easily use different bright colors to highlight certain points and create a permanent record of the discussion. With some masking tape and thumb tacks you can hang up the sheets of easel paper all over the room and actually have more information publicly displayed at a given time than with a chalkboard. Additionally, you can preserve your record of the discussion by simply rolling up the sheets at the end of the discussion and referring to them in the future.

Don't forget to see to it that every discussant has paper and pencil for taking notes during the discussion. People are not able to talk whenever they want to and need to jot down ideas as reminders for their future use. This is especially true if they are performing the roles of periodic summarizer, recapitulator, launcher, logician, recorder, or designated first speaker.

To ensure having a good discussion, you must plan well and carefully. You can use the ten points of planning presented to help you prepare for your discussion. Keep in mind that good planning offers you the foundation for a feeling of confidence, which is contagious. When the discussants catch your confidence and recognize elements of your planning, they will respond positively.

QUESTIONING STRATEGIES FOR THE FIVE TYPES OF DISCUSSION

Questioning Strategy for a Policy Discussion

1. What is your initial (preliminary) stand on the issue at this point?
2. What are the goals about this issue, that is, your desired state of affairs?
3. What are relevant current and past facts on this issue?
4. How would you implement the stand you take?
5. What are the probable consequences of your stand?
6. What would be your position if you were person X?
7. What are some other possible positions to take?
8. What are the probable consequences of these alternatives?
9. In what way is your stand on this issue related to another issue or position you've taken previously?
10. In light of all these points, what final stand do you take on this issue?
11. What are the key reasons for this stand?

Questioning Strategy for a Problem-Solving Discussion

1. What are the essential features and conditions of this problem situation?
2. What do you think is the chief cause(s) of the problem?
3. What are the relevant facts about the problem that are connected with the cause(s) of the problem?
4. What action would solve the problem or remove the conflict?
5. What support do you have that this action would solve the problem or remove the conflict?
6. If we took that action, what else might occur?
7. Based on the points raised what do you conclude is the best

or appropriate way to solve the problem or remove the conflict?

Questioning Strategy for an Explaining Discussion

1. What are the essential features and conditions of this situation?
2. What led to this situation?
3. What generalization, rule, or law is related to this situation?
4. What support do you have that this generalization, rule, or law is true (valid)?
5. What are the relevant facts about this situation that connect it with the generalization, rule, or law?
6. Based on the points made what do you conclude explains why this situation occurred?

Questioning Strategy for a Predicting Discussion

1. What are the essential features and conditions of this situation?
2. Given this situation (that is, given that this situation exists or will exist), what do you think will happen as a result of it?
3. What facts and generalizations support your prediction?
4. What other things might happen as a result of this situation?
5. If the predicted situation occurs, what will happen next?
6. Based on the information and predictions before us, what are the probable consequences you now see?
7. What will lead us from the current situation to the one you've predicted?

Questioning Strategy for a Debriefing Discussion

1. What are some of the specifics that occurred to you during the activity such as events you observed, decisions you made, and feelings you had?
2. What did you learn about the situation, yourself, and other people from this activity?
3. What are the key ideas that this activity teaches us?
4. In what ways are the actions, rules, events, facts, and

outcomes of this activity similar to other parts of your life?
5. In what ways can we change this activity to make it more like the real events? (This question is specifically geared to a role-playing activity and may not apply to other types of activity.)
6. What do you conclude from all of these actions and points made?

4

DISCUSSION SKILLS
Contributing, Crystallizing, and Focusing

LEADING A DISCUSSION, LIKE ANY MULTIFACETED SOCIAL activity, requires a combination of several specific skills. Leading a discussion is not one monolithic activity requiring an ability that some people are born with and others will never have. Rather, discussion leading includes a set of identifiable skills that you and everyone else can learn. This is so whether you are the officially designated leader of a discussion group or a member of a discussion group who has emerged as a leader.

IDENTIFYING DISCUSSION SKILLS

This notion of discussion skills means that leading a discussion is more than a positive attitude and a pipe dream. Saying "Today we'll have a good discussion; I just know it; it's the law of averages; after five bad ones in a row we're due for a good one" won't cause a good discussion to occur. A good discussion will no more occur as a result of making such a statement than saying "I just know that I'll shoot 4 under par in my next golf game" will yield a score of 68. Positive thinking is needed in discussion leading as in golf, but it is far from sufficient. Just as the golfer needs to develop the skills of driving and putting, so, too, do you as discussion leader need to learn certain skills. What is more, the discussion leader needs practice just as the golfer, the violinist, and the ballerina need to practice to hone their performance skills.

To say that discussion leading requires you to employ certain skills means that the activity is an active one. The discussion leader can't just sit back and "let it all happen" the right way. It may appear to an untutored eye that a good discussion leader is "letting it happen." But the truth is that the leader—by carefully employing a few specific skills at opportune, critical moments during the discussion—is conducting the ensemble of participants. The leader's skills serve in the same way as the conductor's baton does which indicates who is to play, when, and how. The discussion leader is active by being constantly attentive, by being prepared to participate when necessary, and by actually interacting with the other discussants.

It is possible to present a rather long list of group leadership skills, as many as twenty.* Though such a list would offer some specificity, it would have the distinct disadvantage of being cumbersome, since it is difficult for the human mind to keep track of so many items at the same time. We can only monitor about seven items at one time,† and it is with this in mind that the list of six discussion skills is offered here. Experience has shown that six essential skills are needed in discussion leadership. As leader, you can easily keep these six skills in mind and mentally monitor them as the discussion proceeds. Six is a manageable amount, and these six below offer you guidance and comprehensiveness at the same time.

---

*For long lists see David W. Johnson and Frank P. Johnson, *Joining Together: Group Theory and Group Skills* (Englewood Cliffs, N.J.: Prentice-Hall, Inc., 1975); Morris K. Lai and others, *Main Field Test Report: Discussing Controversial Issues*, Report A72-12 (San Francisco: Far West Laboratory for Educational Research and Development, 1973); William Fawcett Hill, *Learning Thru Discussion*, rev. ed. (Beverly Hills, Calif.: Sage Publications, 1969); and Kenneth D. Benne and Paul Sheats, "Functional Roles of Group Members," *The Journal of Social Issues*, 4, no. 2 (Spring 1948), 41-49.

†George A. Miller, "The Magical Number Seven, Plus or Minus Two: Some Limits on Our Capacity for Processing Information," *Psychological Review*, 63, no. 2 (March 1956), 81-96.

The six discussion leading skills in alphabetical order‡ are:

1. Contributing
2. Crystallizing
3. Focusing
4. Introducing/Closing
5. Questioning
6. Supporting

In this chapter let us treat the skills of contributing, crystallizing, and focusing. In the next chapter we shall treat the remaining three skills.

THE SKILL OF CONTRIBUTING

When you are *contributing* to the discussion, you are making comments that add to the topic at hand. There are always opportunities for you to contribute to the discussion. There are times when the discussants will request information or an opinion from you. If you deem the information to be essential, then by all means contribute. You must be on guard, however, not to become the easy or sole source of information for the discussants. If you contribute too readily or too frequently, the center of the discussion shifts from the discussants to you. Then you have the limelight and perform the intellectual tasks that rightly belong to the discussants themselves. You must not commit the error of underestimating the abilities and knowledge of the discussants and therefore perform for them. You must show restraint with the skill of contributing.

Sometimes the discussants will request an opinion from you. Unless you feel that giving your opinion at that moment will stymie discussion, you must not dodge the request. Especially if you are an adult working with children or an expert working with lay people, there is an obligation to demonstrate to the discussants what an informed and mature person believes. You

---

‡This is as good a way as any to list and treat these six skills. It would be good to list and treat them as they naturally occur in a discussion. However, that is impossible because there is no natural sequence for planning, leading, and debriefing a discussion.

should take the opportunity to give reasons for your opinion and note that it is a personal one that other people need not share. In this way you serve as a model for the discussants.

You can thus contribute by joining in the interaction from a personal initiative as well as by request. To prevent the possibility of domination, you can follow the principle of waiting for a request. Since the key, however, is to lead by example and to elicit and facilitate contributions from others, the principle of speaking only on request does not guarantee against domination. You must take care to contribute only when the information, idea, or opinion offered is essential to the health of the discussion.

In contributing you make remarks as would any discussant, which may relate to the substantive realm, the social-emotional realm, or the procedural realm of the discussion. (See Chapter 2.)

Substantive Realm

The following extract from an ongoing discussion illustrates how the leader contributes in the substantive realm of the discussion. (The discussion on "Fighting Inflation" is already about 5 minutes old.)

SUE: Well, if that's going to continue for a long time, I just don't know what I'm going to do. Our family income isn't keeping pace.

PAUL: Yeah, it's tough because we're caught, you know, in a spiral. Things cost me more—a pair of tennis shoes costs about $20, so since they're ashamed to charge so much, they call them athletic shoes—and, well, the local plumber charges more to fix a leak in the bathroom faucet, and so you demand more from your boss to be able to pay the plumber, and then your boss charges more for the stuff she sells in her store, and so forth and so forth.

JIM: And you're caught another way, too. To protect yourself you must save money, but the rate of interest at the bank is only 5½ percent. If you save at that rate you lose money 'cause inflation is going up at 17 percent each year. But if you don't save, you've lost, too—when that rainy day comes, and it always does.

NAN: I've always spent my money and not worried about the future much. This way I spend the money when it has the same value as when I earned it. I figure, well, if I saved it, it would be worth less and I couldn't stand spending it later when it wasn't worth as much. But lately, I've been rethinking this whole thing and I tell you the truth, well, I don't know what to do.

PAT (Leader): According to this week's newspaper article the cost of living went up only 7 percent; those people who were able to save by investing in bank certificates or gems or something other than a regular savings account in the bank were not hurt badly or even hurt at all.

JIM: The point is still the same, 17 or 7 percent, I guess it depends which economic report you read. Your point on alternative ways to save—really to invest—is the crucial one. Too many people just stick their money in a savings account and don't seek out better ways to invest—either they're lazy or ignorant—and I use that word in its true sense of meaning.

JULIE: Or scared stiff—I think people are afraid to seek other ways.

In this brief portion the leader performs the skill of contributing by doing two things. First, Pat (the leader) corrects the rate of inflation offered by Jim, and second, Pat suggests alternatives to saving money in a regular bank savings account, which pays a low rate of interest. The leader steps into the flow of the discussion to correct an error by stating the correct increase in the cost of living. Because the leader had planned well for contributing, as mentioned in Chapter 3, this statement comes forth easily. This factual contribution is accepted or at least acknowledged with only a brief comment by Jim. Such factual errors, when not corrected by other discussants and when important to the issue, offer excellent opportunities for the leader to contribute without giving the sense of dominating the discussion.

Thus, the leader felt that a substantive contribution was in order. A critical error about the rate of inflation was made. Since the next speaker ignored the error and once more pursued the idea of saving in a bank, the leader believed that it was necessary to contribute dually—to correct the error and offer alternatives to bank savings accounts.

The leader takes the opportunity to point out that saving money in a bank is but one way to save. This idea then elicits a positive reaction by Jim and also serves as the basis for Julie's subsequent remark. This contribution adds a fresh idea to the discussion and offers a possible way for a person to fight inflation. It may be just what Nan should consider doing because she's about to start saving some of her income.

It may well be that someone else later on would have raised these two points made by Pat. That is to say, the leader's contribution at that given point may not have been all that necessary or critical. There is no way to know that for sure, however. In any case, Pat at that moment made a leadership judgment and performed the skill of contributing.

Social-Emotional Realm

Let us briefly look at another example of contributing in a later excerpt from the same discussion. This time the leader contributes to the social-emotional realm.

> JOE: Excuse me for saying so, but I get the feeling here that everyone is so frustrated about inflation that we can't really think straight—and I'm including myself in this so don't think I'm talking only about you all. Pat, do you get this feeling, too?
>
> PAT (Leader): Yes, I sense a feeling of frustration on everyone's part as I noted before. The answers to inflation don't come easily, and then we get frustrated because we think we should have a fast and easy battle plan. It's O.K. to be frustrated, but as long as we're headed in the right direction, I wouldn't be concerned. Let's keep our senses and proceed with suggestions of alternative ways to combat inflation.

Here, too, the leader contributes by responding to Joe's request. Pat agrees with Joe's sense of the group. Rather than dodge the question or redirect back to the group, Pat decided to respond directly and use the opportunity to calm everyone down after agreeing about a level of frustration. Pat made a leadership decision to contribute to the discussion and felt that a social-emotional contribution was in order. Joe sensed a feeling of frustration and requested that Pat comment on his remarks. Pat chose to contribute in regard to the tone of the discussion.

Procedural Realm

It is possible to contribute in the procedural realm as well as in the substantive and social emotional realms. Below is a short example of the leader contributing in regard to procedures at another part of the discussion on inflation.

> NAN: The more I've been listening the more I've realized that I'd better get myself on track with some kind of plan.
>
> PAT (Leader): At this point we can do one of three things. We can discuss investing in gems, in particular, to aid Nan and anyone else, or we can look at the government's plan to curb inflation by raising interest rates, or we can take a brief historical look at other periods of inflation such as the early 1960s. It's up to you. For what it's worth I think we ought to help Nan and delay the other suggestions for fuller treatment at our next meeting. I can see the advantages of reversing the order, however, and so I'll do what you prefer. Please let me know.

In this utterance Pat identifies a potential fork in the discussion's path. There are three possible ways to proceed and Pat is willing to go with the group's decision. At the same time, it is perfectly clear that the leader has a preference here based on the desire to help Nan, who has a personal and immediate need. Also, the other two possibilities require more time, which will be available at the next meeting. Pat's contribution, the presentation of the three possibilities combined with the statement of preference for the first, does not come at the request of someone but on the leader's own initiative.

Pat has sensed a turning point because of Nan's indirect, almost shy, request for help. Rather than turn away from Nan, Pat reacts by identifying the possibilities while taking the opportunity to show Nan that someone is listening intensely. Pat inserts a preference before asking the group for its opinion because of the desire to influence the decision that relates directly to Nan, a member of the group. For Pat this is significant.

The judgments in the three instances were based on some guidelines concerning the appropriateness and timing for making a contribution to the discussion. These guidelines are as follows:

Guidelines for Performing the Skill of Contributing

1. Provide needed information that other discussants do not contribute themselves.

2. Correct errors that are deemed critical and that other discussants do not correct.
3. Enter the discussion when it is apparent that other discussants will not make a particular point deemed essential.
4. Respond to requests by other discussants.
5. Offer new ways to view a point already raised.
6. Make the contribution brief, allowing the other discussants to be the main contributors. Do not dominate by lengthy or frequent contributions.

Opportunities for Practicing the Skill of Contributing

1. When you're dining with your family or friends, make an effort to listen to the others speak so that you can contribute to the topic at hand. In order for you to be able to contribute significantly, suggest to everyone a topic on which you're moderately or well read. For example, talk about the lead article in the daily newspaper or weekly magazine so that you will be able to contribute at least two or three times.
2. Follow a particular event in the newspaper for a week or so. Then read the related letters to the editor that appear subsequently. For each letter *write* out at least one statement that you can make in reaction to the letter writer, either correcting an error made or offering an alternative viewpoint on the matter.
3. View a television program in which guests are interviewed, such as "Meet the Press." After listening to several remarks of the guest, pretend you are the guest's adviser and offer some additional facts or opinions or explanations that you think will help clarify the guest's position.

THE SKILL OF CRYSTALLIZING

The second discussion leading skill is *crystallizing*. When you crystallize, you state in a concise way the essence of another discussant's remarks or of several remarks in a particular segment of the ongoing interaction. Crystallizing can take the form of a summary where you restate what has been said in a condensed and brief way. More often, crystallizing goes beyond summarizing because you interpret the remarks that have been said in order to get at their implied as well as at their explicit meanings. Crystallizing aims to get at the overall meaning of the messages conveyed and thus requires the leader to be concerned with verbal and nonverbal, intended and unintended, and overt and covert messages.

You can crystallize the discussion by interpreting tone, interpreting content, using analogy, or using a declarative statement or question.

Interpreting Tone

Let us look again at the earlier excerpt from the discussion on "Fighting Inflation." Note the leader's remarks here inserted after Sue and Paul speak.

SUE: Well, if that's going to continue for a long time, I just don't know what I'm going to do. Our family income isn't keeping pace.

PAUL: Yeah, it's tough because we're caught, you know, in a spiral. Things cost me more—a pair of tennis shoes costs about $20, so since they're ashamed to charge so much, they call them athletic shoes—and, well, the local plumber charges more to fix a leak in the bathroom faucet, and so you demand more from your boss to be able to pay the plumber, and then your boss charges more for the stuff she sells in her store, and so forth and so forth.

PAT (Leader): Both Sue and Paul seem to be describing what's going on in our spiraling inflation and also expressing their feelings of frustration and futility.

With this entry into the discussion Pat crystallizes the content of the remarks by Sue and Paul and also interprets the tone of their messages. Pat does not introduce the term "spiral" for Paul has done that. The new terms introduced by Pat are "frustration" and "futility," which were used to get at the essence of the remarks. Sue and Paul, as well as the other discussants, can now use these terms to pursue the source of the frustration and futility, the person, agency, or events associated with the frustration and futility, similar or dissimilar reactions by other people, or any other subtopic of inflation as it relates to such feelings.

Interpreting Content

Pat's crystallizing remarks need not take the above form, however. There obviously is more than one way to crystallize Sue's and Paul's comments. Pat could justifiably have crystallized in the following way:

> PAT (Leader): Sue and Paul are saying that they don't have a personal way to combat inflation. Their incomes aren't increasing as fast as prices. Like Alice in Wonderland they have to run faster just to stay in the same place. Their jobs don't offer the flexible opportunity to earn more when needed; a stagnant income in inflationary times is disastrous.

Note that this second crystallizing comment has a quite different focus from the first one. This second one keeps the focus on the *content* as it introduces the analogy with Alice in Wonderland and the terms "flexible opportunity," "stagnant income," and "disastrous." While the first crystallizing gives a nod to content, the focus there is on the *feelings* expressed by Sue and Paul. The second crystallizing avoids getting involved in the speakers' emotions and hints at possible future directions for the discussion connected with the new terms introduced. Sue and Paul, as well as the other discussants, can now use the terms "flexible opportunity" and "stagnant income" to comment on different types of jobs, who has these jobs, how to get a job that offers flexible opportunity, how to get a job with a flowing rather than a stagnant income, and many other subtopics of inflation concerned with jobs.

The difference between these two possible types of crystallizing, tone and content, is obvious as we read it here in print. The difference in an ongoing discussion is not so readily apparent to the discussants because of the speed and complexity of the interaction. Nevertheless, the impact of each type on a discussion is significant, even though few people realize it at the moment you crystallize. Your crystallizing move is a subtle and powerful one.

Using Analogy

An excellent technique in crystallizing is the use of analogy. An analogy has the power to give a shade of interpretation unrecognized by the discussants until that point. Poets and novelists have long known of and used analogies to offer fresh insights for understanding common events or objects. Note how the leader above used the analogy of Alice in Wonderland to highlight the frustration of someone running just to stay at the same place. Another possibility for using analogy is:

> PAT (Leader): Sue and Paul are saying that they don't have a personal way to combat inflation. Their incomes aren't increasing as fast as prices. It's like a jogger on a treadmill, running a mile at a good clip of eight minutes, but staying in the same spot. Sue and Paul are like joggers on a treadmill.

If not overdone, crystallizing offers you an excellent opportunity to gently highlight key points of a discussion while at the same time gently steering it into new directions. If overused, crystallizing becomes the vehicle by which you dominate the discussion. Like small amounts of sugar in coffee, judicious use of the crystallizing skill can sweeten the discussion; large amounts can make the brew lose its taste.

Using Declarative Statement or Question

Crystallizing, as shown above, can take form of a declarative statement. It can also be phrased as a question. The use of a question format is particularly suited and recommended when you wish to *crystallize the tone* of someone's remarks. For example, in the first example above the leader would better crystallize with a question:

> PAT (Leader): Sue and Paul, you seem to be describing what's going on in our spiraling inflation and you seem to be expressing feelings of frustration and futility. Is this right?

When phrased as a question, crystallizing offers you the opportunity to check back with the speakers to see if your interpretation is correct. It is both safer and less threatening to crystallize the feelings of a discussant with a question than with a statement, for it is often possible to interpret a person's remarks in more than one way. There are many ways to phrase a crystallizing question so as to convey the message, "This is the tone you're manifesting to me. Let me know if I'm putting a correct interpretation on what you've said."

Guidelines for Performing the Skill of Crystallizing

1. Clarify points made by the discussants who may not even be aware of the various messages being sent out to the group.
2. Offer a sharp, alternative way to perceive the meaning of the speakers' remarks.
3. Reflect to the group what the impact of their remarks is.
4. Remind everyone of what is the kernel of the remarks being made.
5. Indicate to speakers that, though you as leader are not speaking much, you are listening attentively.

Opportunities for Practicing the Skill of Crystallizing

1. Listen to a television interview program. After the guest responds to a question from the interviewer, turn off the sound. *Crystallize the content* of the guest's remarks in two or three sentences.
2. Make a list of items, such as hobbies, sports, plays, songs, books, and people, with which you are familiar. Choose one item to focus on. Then as you hear family and friends talking, think of an appropriate analogy based on that item. Stick with a particular item until you're satisfied that you've come up with an analogy based on it. A good format to use is: What you're saying reminds me of _____.
3. Listen to or read the text of a speech by a politician or an official of a large organization. At two points during the speech *crystallize the tone* of the speaker.

THE SKILL OF FOCUSING

The third discussion leading skill is *focusing*. Every discussion goes astray at least once somewhere along the line. Most of the time the drift is gradual—someone speaks about item A, someone comments on item B which is related to A, then someone makes point C which is related to B, and so forth. When you *focus* the discussion, you put the discussion on its intended course or direct it onto another path that is deemed desirable.

Once again, let us look at a part of the discussion on "Fighting Inflation." We pick it up during Jim's second remark to see where the leader can use the focusing skill.

> JIM: Too many people just stick their money in a savings account and don't seek out better ways to invest—either they're lazy or ignorant—and I use that word in its true sense of meaning.
> JULIE: Or scared stiff—I think people are afraid to seek other ways.
> PAT (Leader): Let's concentrate on alternatives to a savings account in a bank. Please suggest a series of alternatives now.

What Pat has done here is focus the discussion. The discussants will now not concern themselves with the inflation spiral directly but with alternative ways of saving so as to gain more income through higher interest. Pat has heard the comment about alternatives to a bank savings account and decided that, because of the interest and need expressed by Sue, Paul, and Julie, it would be beneficial to list what is possible for them to do. This decision by Pat is a deliberate move to focus the discussion.

As with all of the other skills there are several ways to focus. Pat could have said something like, "Since alternative ways to saving are important as a way of keeping pace, please address yourselves to this point for the time being." Such a focusing statement would indicate not only the direction to be taken but also connect the direction with previous remarks by using the very language used earlier, "keeping pace." To be even more specific and give a longer focus, Pat could add, "And let's try to identify at least six alternatives to a bank savings account." This would indicate to the discussants what Pat expects before being willing to focus again.

Focusing at this point also serves an indirect function that deserves attention here briefly. By even slightly changing the direction of the discussion Pat removes Jim from the center of the interaction and permits other people to talk. (We shall treat this function of the leader more fully later when we examine the sixth discussion skill, supporting.)

Not only are there several ways to focus, but at almost every juncture there are several different directions a discussion can take. Even though you have a general plan in mind and thus know the basic direction for the discussion, there are always many points where there is need for focusing. A precise focus for a discussion can never be 100 percent predetermined. No plan can foresee the myriad of opportunities that arise once the discussants begin talking.

For example, after Julie spoke in our illustrative discussion, Pat focused on alternative ways. But Pat could have also focused on the reasons and feelings connected with the alternatives, as suggested by Jim and Julie. Pat could have said:

> Let's turn to the reasons for the popularity of savings accounts in banks despite their low interest rate.
>
> or
>
> Let's turn our attention for a few minutes to feelings or attitudes people have about alternative ways to save—Jim said "lazy" and Julie said "scared stiff." This will help us understand perhaps the overall effect of inflation on people.
>
> or
>
> Let's not shift to alternative savings possibilities because that will distract us from considering the causes and effects of a spiraling inflation. Our focus should now still be on the causes of inflation, and then we'll pick up the effects shortly.

Note two important elements in the three alternative focusing statements above. In the second and third statements, the leader gives reasons for focusing whereas in the first one no reason is given. In the second alternative Pat states, "This will help us understand . . ." and in the third alternative says, ". . . because that will distract us from considering causes and effects of a spiraling inflation." The leader doesn't need to give reasons but can and should if there is any hint of resistance to the direction given or there is a desire to keep everyone posted at all times.

Another noteworthy element appears in the third alternative. Here the leader focuses by giving a negative statement. Pat states what is not allowable. Such a negative, or exclusionary, statement indicates what is not to be discussed, and it is important and permissible. But since a negative statement does not suffice to tell the discussants what to focus on, Pat correctly adds on a positive statement so as to clarify matters for everyone.

In each of the three alternative focusing statements given above the discussion would take a different though connected path. Which is the correct or best path to take at a given point depends on you, the needs of the discussants, and your overall plan for the discussion. In any case, the decision is made quickly on the spur of the moment because no discussion plan can account for every focusing opportunity ahead of time.

Guidelines for Performing the Skill of Focusing

1. Keep the discussion going along planned directions so that there can be progress rather than mere "spinning of wheels."
2. Set limits on what can be discussed and what is considered to be "off-limits."
3. Provide for needs of the discussants as they arise in connection with the overall discussion plan.
4. Provide opportunity to allow some silent or verbally inactive discussants to participate as well as to gently remove a dominant speaker from the limelight.

Opportunities for Practicing the Skill of Focusing

1. When you're dining with your family or friends, listen carefully with the intent of focusing their remarks at least twice. Each time pick up on a new idea introduced that you think should be talked about a bit more. A helpful format for you to use is: "You've brought up a good point about _____. I think we ought to talk about that some more. Would you elaborate on that, please."
2. Listen to a television interview program. Pretend that you are the interviewer. After you have heard the guest make some

initial remarks, make a focusing statement that includes a negative statement prohibiting talk about a particular aspect of the topic at hand.
3. When you're talking with family or friends, focus the talk in such a way that it will involve someone who is being somewhat shy or untalkative. Focus the talk so as to induce that person to participate more.

This chapter shows that the three discussion skills of contributing, crystallizing, and focusing are essential to you as discussion leader. You don't need to perform any one of these skills often in order to influence the discussion. An appropriate contribution or crystallizing statement can have a strong impact even though the discussants may not realize it. A focusing statement, on the other hand, is a much more direct way of influencing the direction of the discussion. The key with these three skills is to remember not to use them so much that you dominate the discussion.

5

DISCUSSION SKILLS
Introducing/Closing, Questioning, and Supporting

THE NEXT THREE DISCUSSION LEADERSHIP SKILLS ARE LAST simply by coincidence of the English language. Introducing/ Closing, Questioning, and Supporting come after Contributing, Crystallizing, and Focusing in the alphabet. For this reason we have an apparently odd situation where the second chapter dealing with discussion skills and not the first begins with Introducing/Closing. This, however, only highlights the importance of all six discussion skills.

THE SKILL OF INTRODUCING/CLOSING

The fourth discussion leadership skill is introducing/closing. Introducing and closing are almost symmetrical skills, and what can be said of one pertains quite closely to the other; hence, they are discussed here as one skill. With this two-fold skill you as leader can effectively introduce the discussion so it can get off the ground and you later can close it so the discussants have a sense of satisfaction about what they did. Sometimes discussion fails to get moving because a leader has failed to introduce the topic properly; and sometimes discussants leave without a feeling of satisfaction and closure even though they have achieved their purpose.

The Skill of Introducing

A key element in introducing a discussion is brevity. People gathered around a table or seated in a room or under a tree generally expect to talk and want to talk. Your task is to introduce the discussion briefly in such a way as to say, "We're here to discuss, so let's do it; I don't plan to be, and I won't be, the dominant speaker."

Let us turn to the leader's remarks at the beginning of the discussion on "Fighting Inflation" to see how it was introduced.

> PAT (Leader): We're going to discuss inflation. Specifically, we're initially interested in the question that gives us both sides of the coin, "What are the causes and effects on us, collectively and individually, of our inflationary situation today?" At our last meeting we decided that we will look at the *effects* and *then* the *causes*—for a change from the usual. So we'll start with that. Later we'll cope with how to fight inflation individually.

In this brief introduction Pat has accomplished several things within just a few seconds—it took about thirty seconds to make this introduction. Pat has stated what the topic is—inflation— and what aspects of it the group will discuss. The discussants within one-half a minute can begin to participate. Since it is a topic of interest to everyone, they will not sit frustrated as the leader expounds on the intricacies of an inflationary economy or personal gripes about the consequences of inflation. By being brief Pat has notified everyone that this will be a group discussion and not a personal "soap box" opportunity.

Using a Question. The leader has notified everyone that the topic is inflation, in general. Then Pat has clarified the topic by stating a specific question about inflation. Everyone now knows that the group will discuss the effects of inflation rather than the president's policy about inflation. The use of a question in introducing a discussion is the best and the recommended way for clarifying the topic. A question provides precision and clarity, qualities which are absolutely necessary, and at the same time a question evokes a response and gets the discussion going.

The leader has asked a direct question, which is obvious, in introducing the discussion. There is also an indirect question, which is not so obvious at first glance. This indirect question is signaled by the words "how to" and thus we have the indirect question, "later we'll cope with how to fight inflation individually." The direct question is more precise and clearer than the indirect one, and this is as it should be. Since the indirect question is the second question and the one to be dealt with later on, there is no problem here now. With these two questions the leader succeeds in introducing the topic effectively. Pat can ask a specific direct question later or can turn to that subtopic by using the focusing skill at the appropriate time.

Unless the nature of the topic is clear to the discussants, the leader will create verbal chaos or will thwart the desire to speak that everyone has. Without clarity the discussion cannot get off the ground because no one knows what to talk about. Few people wish to put themselves out on a limb and talk about something that may be regarded as being off-target. Few people wish to be corrected or told that they've just misinterpreted the topic, whether or not they have.

Note also that the question posed in the introduction calls for many possible responses. It is obvious from the way the leader phrased the question that there is not just one right answer that is expected from the group. Many people will need to speak and each one will have to say more than a word or two. It is for this purpose—the encouragement of substantial contributions by discussants—that the leader did not pose the questions in a yes/no form.

Procedural Issues. Especially in large groups, and also in small groups coming together for the first time, it is necessary to add one more element to the introducing. This is the element of procedure. As you introduce the topic for discussion, you must make it clear to everyone how you will proceed. For example, will the discussion begin by anyone responding to the question?

Or, will it begin by having an expert with a prepared statement take an opening position? Or, will it begin by someone reviewing the contents of a movie or a play familiar to all the discussants?

In general, it is best for you to pose the procedural question to the group. Let them decide how they will begin. In this way, as in the choice of topic, the discussants have a stake—owner-ship—in the procedure. Obviously, you can contribute your own suggestion but yours will be only one among others from which the group can choose.

Let us tie this procedural element of introducing to the clarify-ing element presented earlier. Note how one flows into the other.

> PAT (Leader): We're going to discuss inflation. Specifically, we're initially interested in the question that gives us both sides of the coin, "What are the causes and effects on us, collectively and individually, of our inflationary status?" At our last meeting we decided that we will look at the effects and then the causes—for a change from the usual. So we'll start with that. Later we'll cope with how to fight inflation individually. Now, let's quickly decide how we'll proceed. We have several options already, and the floor is open for more. We can get going as we did last time by simply opening the floor up for responses to our question of "What are the effects of inflation?" or we can ask our guest to make an initial comment about the newspaper article we all read or we can do something else that you suggest. What do you think?

Here Pat moves directly to the procedural issue before entertain-ing any answers to the key question. The question for discussion is clear, and the group last time decided to talk about effects before causes. But since the group has made no prior decision about procedure, Pat wisely raises the question. Moreover, as leader, Pat offers two possibilities for the group to consider plus the option of adding other possibilities. Now the discussants must decide how to proceed. It will be *their* decision, and they will establish ownership. This is most important for smooth progress in the future.

After a *brief* set of exchanges and a decision on procedure by the group, it is advisable for you to briefly make a summary of what the question for discussion is and the way the group will proceed. You can do all of this in a short period of time and then begin discussing the topic. Keep the pace lively but deal with the procedural issue *before* permitting substantive interaction.

Sometimes you will pose a yes/no question when introducing the topic. This may occur because the question was framed by someone else and could not be changed. Or, the topic is one which deals with a policy issue and you wish to elicit a short response from everyone as a way of demonstrating the lack of unanimity in the group. Or, you wish to diagnose the group's preferences. If you do pose a yes/no question, then there will be a need immediately following the initial responses for you to focus the discussion. For example:

> LEADER: Today we're going to discuss whether the government should provide programs for minority groups that favor them in housing and employment. The question posed on the flyer you received in the mail is, "Should the government favor minorities (for example, Blacks, Chicanos, Orientals) when hiring new employees for itself or in federally financed projects?"
>
> JONATHAN: Absolutely
>
> LEADER: Ruth?
>
> RUTH: Yes
>
> ANNE: Yes
>
> JILL: No
>
> JIM: Yes
>
> RACHEL: No
>
> LEADER: We've heard from everyone, and it's clear that we all don't agree. As a way of examining the advantages and disadvantages of such a policy, I suggest that we explore the probable consequences of having the government favor minority groups. That is, "What are the probable consequences?" How shall we proceed to answer that question. One possibility is to have Jill and Anne respond first since this will give us replies from different perspectives. What is your choice on procedure?

Whether you consider the leader's second statement above as part of the introduction or as an example of the use of the focusing skill is not critical here. You could easily make a case for either claim because of the nature of the situation. The critical point is the leader's recognition of the need to ask the second question on probable consequences. Without it there can be no discussion. By having everyone respond to the advance question, the leader was able to diagnose the group's opinions on favoring minorities as well as have everyone participate early in the discussion. With the second question the topic for discussion becomes clear, and exchanges among members of the group can begin once the group decides on procedure.

The Skill of Closing

The skill of *closing* a discussion is the most overlooked and undervalued one. Most people are so drained by the strain of leading a discussion that they simply pay little attention to the need for an effective closing. Or, they are so happy or so disappointed about how the discussion progressed that they don't care how the discussion ends. "Ending" a discussion and "closing" a discussion are not synonyms at all. Every discussion must "end" at one time or another, but an ending does not guarantee closure. A discussion might end because the time allowed for it has expired or because a fire interrupted it. A discussion closes when someone takes deliberate steps.

When you close a discussion, you recapitulate (or provide for a recapitulation of) the key points of the discussion and then you launch the group into what it has decided to do next. If the group itself hasn't decided "where it wants to go from here," then you have the obligation to make suggestions for the future in terms of further group activities or further individual follow-up projects. In either case, the group gets a sense of what is coming in light of what it has done. There is a sense of harmony and closure. Closing is important to a discussion just like a coda is important to a symphony. A discordant coda can ruin the listener's sense of satisfaction just as a poor closing can ruin the effect of a discussion no matter how good the interaction among members was.

Recapitulating and Launching. Let us look at the ending segment of the discussion on "Fighting Inflation" to see how the leader uses the skill of closing.

ELANA: What you've said, especially Jim and Alice, makes a lot of sense to me. I still don't know if I have the strength to fight back, because it seems to me, you know, that it's one constant battle. O.K., I'll try to invest in gems or at least artworks—I have a good feel for them—but I don't know if I have the courage to become active in our union to strengthen its bargaining power.

PAT (Leader): Well, our time is just about up. We've hit on four excellent points today: (1) inflation tends to spiral; (2) we generally feel anxious in the face of rising prices; (3) we're all caught by inflation but the ones caught worst are those with a steady income; and (4) we should try to find opportunities for a flexible income and alternative ways to invest that yield higher returns than savings accounts in banks, such as investing in gems, paintings, stocks and bonds, and real estate. Let me suggest then that when you leave you do two things. First, reexamine your own current method of fighting inflation. Second, based on your examination, list three first steps you can easily take in order to fight back. Next week we can begin by asking for volunteers to tell us the three steps they've come up with. Do you have any suggestions for our future meeting?

The leader above closes effectively by first recapitulating and then launching the group into the future. Without this closing move, the discussion would end abruptly and without its coda. Furthermore, with only the recapitulating element or with only the launching element, the closing would be incomplete and inadequate. To see this point, read aloud the statement by Elana and then just the recapitulating part or the launching part. With both elements in the closing the discussion ends in a satisfying way. The discussants know that they have finished and where they are going next.

The leader here recapitulates only the substantive points of the discussion. It is possible to include procedural elements and social-emotional elements as well. It is a matter of judgment, then, as to what are the high points of the discussion. While it is possible to omit the procedural and social-emotional high points (although often such an omission would be an error), it is incorrect to omit the substantive ones. After all, a discussion must be about something and some key points arise in every discussion.

The launching element by the leader after the recapitulation deserves careful attention. The leader has launched everyone to *do* something, something more than just talking again. It is important to launch an activity for discussants to *do*. The leader here ties the activity to a future discussion as well and cleverly links the discussion, the interim activity, and a future discussion together. In this way the future naturally springs from the present.

The leader also makes another noteworthy move by weaving in a compliment to the group. The leader specifically mentions the "excellent" points of the discussion. We shall treat this idea further when we deal with the supporting skill shortly.

Three more points about the closing deserve attention. One, the closing by Pat gives a feeling of firmness so that the discussants know for sure that talk won't start up again. It is important that once the discussion enters its closing stage and the discussants set their minds to future activities, the interaction doesn't begin anew. If it does, there arises an unsettling feeling and a drain on everyone's intellectual and emotional resources. Two, the closing is brief, taking only about a minute. Just as it is important to be brief when introducing a discussion, it is important to be brief when closing so that the discussion still belongs to the group and not the leader. The leader ought not to capitalize on the silence of the discussants during the "coda" to expound at length on the topic from a personal perspective.

Three, the leader closes this discussion when the time allotted to it ends. The leader allows a minute or two for the closing. Sometimes you will close a discussion when it is evident that the discussants are not able to continue due to lack of intellectual or emotional energy, interest, or ability. The preferred time to end, though it is not always possible to do so, occurs when the discussants have reached conclusions indicating the achievement of the goals of the discussion. The two conditions of (1) the loss of energy, interest, or ability and (2) the achievement of goals require you to make a careful decision about closing. The decision to close or not is reached by consulting your discussion plan and assessing the state of affairs in the room. In contrast, there is little judgment involved when closing because time has run out.

An excellent way to close a discussion is to ask a discussant to do the recapitulating. Since it is difficult for most discussants to do this—primarily because they have not had practice doing so—it is most often necessary to set the stage for a participant recapitulating at the very start of the discussion. You can ask someone to take the role of discussion recorder and then ask the recorder to "*briefly* recapitulate" based on the notes taken all along. Or, you can speak with someone before the discussion begins. Or, at the very beginning of the interaction, you can alert a person to be ready to recapitulate at the end of the discussion. A summary statement by a discussant is most valuable. Planning with someone to do this is a good idea. For example:

> PAT (Leader): Well, our time is just about up and Jerry volunteered earlier with me to mention the high points as he sees them. So, Jerry, go ahead, and then we'll see where we go from here.

After the recapitulation, whether by a discussant or by you, the launching must still come. This, as shown above, can be by you or someone else. You can arrange for a launcher before the discussion begins. Or, you can move into the launching phase by raising a question to the group. If this tack is taken, then you must raise the question early enough to permit several responses which the discussants can talk about and around which they can come to an agreement. For example:

> PAT (Leader): Thanks very much, Jerry, for your concise and astute remarks. Now, let's determine where we go from here. Are there any related activities to "Fighting Inflation" which you'd like to do as a follow-up of today's discussion?

What follows from this closing question will be ideas to launch the discussants into the future. They may be quite different from the activity chosen by you. Since they come from the discussants themselves, they probably will be right on target in regard to their needs and interests. Thus, just as you can recapitulate or provide for someone else to do so, you can launch new activities, provide for someone else to do so, or elicit suggested activities for the future. Whatever the path taken, you must close the discussion.

Guidelines for Performing the Skill of Introducing/Closing

1. Be brief.
2. Initiate the interaction by clarifying the topic and subtopic for discussion.

3. Clarify the specific topic for discussion with a question that provides for a set of responses to be talked about by the discussants.
4. Raise the question of procedure, and ask the discussants to make the decision before substantive exchanges begin.
5. In closing the discussion recapitulate the high points and launch future activities.
6. Close when the allotted time ends, or when the discussants' attention lapses, or preferably when the discussants have achieved their goal.

Opportunities for Practicing the Skill of Introducing/Closing

1. Follow a particular event in the newspaper for a week or so. Then pretend you are leading a discussion with a group of seven journalists. Prepare your introducing remarks to be about 50 to 60 seconds. Include an explicit question not in yes/no form and several suggestions for procedure. Time the length of your remarks by reading them aloud. If need be, revise your remarks.
2. View a television program where a panel discusses an issue. As the program time runs out, turn off the sound, and assume the task of closing the discussion. Try to recapitulate all three realms (substantive, social-emotional, and procedural), and launch some new activities for the panelists.
3. Prepare an introduction to a political topic that includes a question in yes/no form. Then assume that *all* the discussants answer yes to the question. Suggest two procedures to the group so that discussion can begin among them.

THE SKILL OF QUESTIONING

The fifth discussion leading skill is *questioning*.* The purpose of questioning by you is to involve the discussants and to bring forth needed data, opinions, explanations, and generalizations. A given question can and often does serve several legitimate

---

*For an in-depth treatment of the concept and skill of questioning, see Ronald T. Hyman, *Strategic Questioning* (Englewood Cliffs: N.J.: Prentice-Hall, 1979).

purposes simultaneously. We have already seen how questions are often an integral element in the skill of focusing.† In leading a discussion you ask questions to the general group and to particular discussants so that the flow of the discussion can proceed.

Let us look at an excerpt from the discussion, "Fighting Inflation," where questioning is not part of focusing but has another purpose.

> DAVID: Another way to save and invest money is to buy gems. (Pause)
>
> PAT (Leader): David, would you please be more specific and give us some examples of saving money by buying gems.

Probing

With this question the leader probes David's remark about investing in gems. Pat asks David to give specifics about gems. David might well reply, "You could invest in diamonds, or emeralds, or rubies, or sapphires. These are the best-known precious gems." David's original contribution to alternative ways of saving is somewhat vague, and the leader judged it important to bring out onto the floor the types of gems people can buy instead of putting their money into a bank savings account. Pat probes to elicit specificity and thus remove the vagueness of "to buy gems."

There are many types of probing questions. This particular probe for specifics came out because the leader believed it necessary to move deeper into an area already raised by a discussant. A probe need not be aimed at the person making the initial remark though most often it is.

There are probes that ask for

1. specifics
2. clarification of an idea
3. consequences of a suggested course of action
4. elaboration of a point

---

†In a sense every remark made by a discussant helps to focus the discussion. But the skill of focusing refers to statements that explicitly serve to announce to everyone the direction that the discussion will take.

5. parallel cases
6. implementation of a proposed idea
7. relationships to other issues
8. comments from the perspective of another person (the role-switch probe)
9. explanation of how the discussant arrived at the position taken
10. explanation of reasons (causes or purposes) of a suggested idea

The leader must decide which probe to use at any given time. The most common probe is "Why?" that elicits reasons for an event or an opinion. Other less popular probes are most often preferable. Not only do they offer a change of pace but they also add a new dimension that can propel a discussion forward. Notice the difference between two possible probing questions at this point in the discussion:

PAUL: I believe that the government should advise small investors.
LEADER Probe A: Why do you believe this?
LEADER Probe B: What would be the consequences if the government set up such an advisory service?

Whereas Probe A gets at reasons for holding the stated opinion and thus leads to support of the *preceding* opinion, Probe B seeks the probable results of such an action and thus looks *to the future*. To add spice and challenge to the discussion you should use a variety of probes. Each of the ten probes listed above offers a unique flavor to the discussion. This is evident when any of them is asked after Paul's opinion about the government advising small investors.

There is one caution you must heed when probing. Be careful to avoid threatening the discussant. Ask your question in a way that indicates that you are seeking information rather than putting the person on the spot or embarrassing him or her. Also, choose a probe that suits the discussant. For example, most people will find the "How-did-you-arrive-at-that-opinion" probe? (which examines process) less threatening than the "Why-do-you-hold-that-opinion" probe (which examines personal justification). In general, the least threatening of all is the "clarification" probe with "consequences" close behind it. Your knowledge of the group and your experience with it will help here. A helpful rule of thumb is to avoid the "why" probe on policy or personal matters in favor of other, less threatening probes.

Bringing Forth Information

Other questions which you ask do not seek to probe so much as to bring forth data, opinions, explanations, or generalizations. In listening to the remarks of the discussants you sense the need for some additional data or the drawing of a generalization.

> JULIE: It's also possible to save by investing in real estate. You can buy land on your own or you can purchase shares in some syndicate that owns a shopping center or hotel. Real estate offers high return on your money, too, these days.
> PAT (Leader): What conclusion do you draw from these last few statements about gems, stocks and bonds, artworks, and real estate?

Here the leader senses the need for a generalization drawn from the previous remarks. This will serve as an antidote to the fear and frustration people feel because they don't know how to save except for putting their money away in a savings account in the bank. Though the discussants have heard all the alternatives individually, the leader believes that one comprehensive statement in the form of a generalization will add strength to the various suggestions for fighting inflation. To elicit the generalization, the leader asks for it.

Questioning is without a doubt an essential discussion leading skill. Its power lies in the fact that the discussants recognize the expectation to respond to a question. It is impossible to conceive of leading a discussion without asking a question. (A question need not be stated in the interrogative form; it may be in any grammatical form. The key to recognizing a question is the fact that it expects a response. Thus, as given in an earlier excerpt, "Please suggest a series of alternatives now" is a question as far as discussion leading is concerned.) But despite the necessity for questioning, it is clear that you should perform other skills, too. If you only ask questions, the discussion will suffer, and the discussants will conceive of you as interrogator rather than as leader.

You must also take care not to inject many questions into the discussion. If you ask many questions, the discussants will find themselves responding to you most of the time. You will dominate the discussion by your questions and their many responses. The discussants need an opportunity to talk to each other, to embellish a point already made, to agree with it, to disagree with it, and to raise their own questions.

For this reason, it is important that you plan your key questions ahead of time, keeping them to a minimum and asking them only when they haven't been asked by someone else. It may be necessary for you to monitor your questioning behavior because most people ask many more questions than they realize. You may find it helpful or necessary to tape record yourself as leader and listen to the playback in order to learn how you sound and to examine the questions you asked.

Guidelines for Performing the Skill of Questioning

1. Question when data, opinions, explanations, and generalizations are needed for the flow of the discussion
2. Probe when further points will add to the topic for other discussants to build on
3. Question with a tone that expresses a seeking of information
4. Avoid threatening and embarrassing the respondent
5. Mix questioning with other discussion skills so as to avoid the label of interrogator
6. After asking a question, pause to allow time for people to respond; allow at least four seconds before speaking again

Opportunities for Practicing the Skill of Questioning

1. Read an editorial in a newspaper on an event that you have been following. Ask two different probing questions to the writer, other than a "why" question.

2. When you're dining with family or friends, listen carefully to their remarks. After approximately five minutes ask someone to make a generalization based on what they've been talking about.
3. Read a newspaper article or listen to a television newscast. After reading or listening to a particular item ask a question eliciting data that will help you understand the event better.

THE SKILL OF SUPPORTING

The sixth discussion leading skill is *supporting*. When you encourage the discussants with words or statements of praise, relieve tension building up in the group by making a humorous remark or mollifying statement, and elicit participation of shy or inactive members by request or nonverbal action, you are *supporting* the discussion. The skill of supporting is always appropriate before, during, and after the discussion and is as much a nonverbal skill as it is a verbal one.

In the discussion we have been using for illustrative purposes, the leader used the supporting skill several times. The various discussants probably didn't realize it though their actions show the effects. For example, the very participation of Sue is outstanding, for Sue was generally quiet and withdrawn during most previous discussions. Recognizing this, the leader arranged to chat with her before the discussion began and sat near her during the discussion. By sitting near her, Pat was able to make eye contact and to exchange smiles with her so as to make Sue feel comfortable, warm, and valued by the leader. Sue reacted positively to these supporting actions by participating more than she had.

In an excerpt cited earlier the leader picked up a point made by Jim and seconded by Julie:

PAT (Leader): Let's concentrate on Jim's point—on alternatives to a savings account in a bank. Please suggest a series of alternatives now.

With this focusing move Pat has nonverbally conveyed the

message to everyone, especially Jim, that Jim's contribution was important. The group is now following up on his point in depth. The message sent to Jim is, "You're doing fine. Your point is well taken. Keep up the good work." Pat thus supports Jim.

Both of the examples above are nonverbal ones. It is also through explicit verbal remarks that the leader supports the discussants. Let us recall first the praise of the leader to the whole group in a closing statement.

> PAT (Leader): Well, our time is just about up. You've hit on four *excellent* points today. . . .

Though this may seem small and appear to go unnoticed, the praise here to the group is important. The leader deliberately inserts praise. All too often people restate what has been said but fail to take the opportunity to support the group. Consider how this statement by Pat would sound and affect the discussants without an element of support in it.

> PAT (Leader): Well, our time is just about up. You've made the following points today about inflation. . . .

The difference is subtle but significant and not to be underestimated.

Let us turn to yet another example of use of the supporting skill done explicitly.

> PAT (Leader): Julie, perhaps you could offer an alternative to savings in a bank from your perspective since we know of your family's business interest.
>
> JULIE: It's also possible to save by investing in real estate. You can buy land on your own or you can purchase shares in some syndicate that owns a shopping center or hotel. Real estate offers high return on your money, too, these days.

Here the leader specifically requests Julie to participate. Others have suggested alternatives to saving in a bank. The leader notices that Julie hasn't contributed an alternative, although she is a natural to do so since her family is involved in a real estate agency and development business. To involve her in a supportive way the leader requests her contribution and gives her a clue about what to say. Pat says that the alternative is related to Julie's "family's business." This request for participation and the clue make it easy for Julie to contribute. She need not break into the interaction and compete with talkative group members. She knows that the floor is hers, that she is expected to contribute an alternative, and that the alternative is related to real estate. With this use of the supporting skill Pat has successfully involved Julie in the discussion.

Seating Arrangement

In the ways illustrated above and in other ways as well, you as the leader can and must use the supporting skill. You must provide for a seating arrangement that facilitates exchanges among the discussants. Discussants should be able to establish eye contact with each other easily. They should be able to hear each other easily. A row-behind-row arrangement of chairs is obviously not one suited to support reluctant speakers. Neither is a long narrow table when the reluctant person is seated far away from you. In a small group (5 to 7 members) a circle or an around-the-table arrangement is best. In a larger group (8 or more members) a semicircle or horseshoe arrangement with you seated in the open space is the best arrangement.

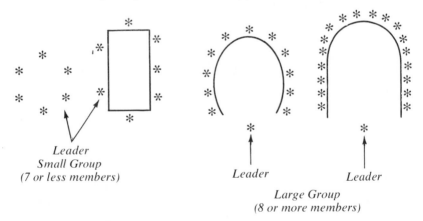

Leader
Small Group
(7 or less members)

Leader   Leader

Large Group
(8 or more members)

It is important not to have "isolates," discussants who sit outside the seating arrangement and cause everyone discomfort in talking and listening to them. Therefore, provide for enough seats and enough room for each person to be an integral part of the group. If necessary, request isolates to sit in the interaction zone. If necessary, prepare a seating arrangement before the discussion begins and seat people accordingly. A discussion is held by a *group talking together*, not by a collection of individuals.

Listening Attentively

An excellent way to demonstrate your support for a discussant is to listen attentively. By active and attentive listening you demonstrate that what the person is saying is important; it is worth listening to. You demonstrate that you care. Since silence is not the same as attentive listening, you can show support by —

1. facing the speaker;
2. making eye contact or focusing on the speaker slightly below the eyes (by doing the latter, you lessen the possibility of making a person nervous);
3. leaning or bending slightly toward the speaker;
4. taking some notes on important points that you should refer to later as a reinforcement of their importance;
5. waiting 3 to 5 seconds after the discussant finishes speaking so as to indicate that you have not just been sitting and waiting desperately to talk; by waiting you show that you are now considering the speaker's message before you proceed.

Keep in mind that a discussion needs listeners as well as speakers. It is difficult—if not impossible—to speak if you feel that no one is listening to you. All speakers constantly modify their messages in light of the feedback they receive from their listeners. Communication is more than Rachel talking and Anne listening and then Anne talking while Rachel listens. What Rachel says depends on Anne; that is, if and how Anne listens. Rachel gets nonverbal feedback from Anne and shapes her messages in light of that feedback that she interprets as she speaks.‡

---

‡Herbert A. Thelen, *Dynamics of Groups at Work* (Chicago: University of Chicago Press, 1954), p. 185.

Communication is complex, and whether we realize it or not, the listener influences the speaker. So, as leader, since you have influence, you might as well make that influence supportive.

Making and Breaking Eye Contact

Making eye contact is a sign of attention to the speaker. Consider how you feel when someone you're talking to looks down at your shoes, or looks away out the window, or looks at your waist. Speakers need and desire eye contact. If in a discussion you are talking to Ruth, for example, and Ruth breaks eye contact with you, you will naturally seek out someone else with whom to establish eye contact. As leader you can use this idea of making and breaking eye contact to help involve other people in the discussion. Suppose you find that Linda talks always and only to you. After you have made eye contact with her, you can gently and politely break eye contact with Linda by looking at the paper on which you take notes. This will induce Linda to establish eye contact with another discussant, who will now be more directly involved in the interaction. Let us assume that Linda makes contact with Charles. Most often, Charles will be the next person to speak since Linda may ask a direct question to him or say something special to him that will lead him to react to Linda's remarks. Thus, breaking eye contact offers you a way to leave the focal point of the discussion and at the same time to involve other discussants in the interaction.

Supporting Discussants after the Discussion

After the discussion ends, you still have the obligation and opportunity to use the skill of supporting. Speak with the discussants individually, especially those who need extra support. Commend them for their contributions so as to reinforce their action. "The point you raised about the need for alternatives to savings accounts in banks as a way of fighting inflation was right on target—it hit the bull's eye" would be appropriate to say to Jim. Thank the discussants and commend them for what they said and how they acted so that they will learn good discussion behavior and be more likely to perform well in a future discussion.

Guidelines for Performing the Skill of Supporting

1. Listen attentively to the other discussants and be patient.
2. Praise the discussants for their good remarks and cooperative actions.
3. Reduce or eliminate growing tension with humor or approval of humor by another discussant (the age-old technique of comic relief).
4. Encourage discussants before, during, and after the discussion proper.
5. Use nonverbal techniques related to room environment, seating arrangement, proximity, eye contact, and body language to demonstrate warmth, encouragement, and harmony.
6. Facilitate participation by shy or inactive discussants with a request, giving specific clues so as to indicate clearly your expectations as well as your understanding.

Opportunities for Practicing the Skill of Supporting

1. Pretend you are scheduled to lead a discussion in your living room. List any four people you will invite to attend and participate. Draw a diagram showing where you will seat the four people and yourself so as to facilitate your discussion.
2. When you're dining with family or friends, select one person in particular whom you will support nonverbally. Plan and use three different nonverbal means of supporting that person. Carefully note what happens as a result of your efforts.
3. View a television panel discussion. After a few minutes select one person of the panel, preferably the least active one, to support. As the program progresses, make explicit pertinent encouraging remarks to that person as a sign of your support.

6

PREVENTING AND SOLVING DISCUSSION PROBLEMS

In some discussions one person or two begins to impede the smooth flow of interaction. Sometimes the disruption is so great that the discussion breaks down and either the discussants disband or they merely spin their wheels as frustration mounts. No discussion leader looks forward to opposition and obstruction. Yet disruptions often occur because leaders do not take definite steps to prevent negative behavior and because they don't know how to deal with it if it does arise. In this chapter we shall deal with your obligation as leader to deal with disruption in four different ways—taking preventive action before the discussion begins, taking preventive action during the discussion, applying a "Band-Aid cure" to minor disruptions, and seeking strong action if major disruption arises.

TYPES OF DISRUPTIVE BEHAVIOR

Let us take a look at several instances of disruptive behavior to clarify the issue before us.

(Discussion: "How can we improve the Olympic Games?")

JACK: What's a shame is the commercialization of the Olympics. It's gotten to be big business instead of good sports.

LARRY: You're a fine one to talk, Jack. What do you know about sports? You haven't played with a ball or run on a track in your whole life. That's a hot one—Jack, the Olympics expert.

Sarcastic, Attacking, and Aggressive Behavior

Larry attacks Jack in a sarcastic tone, berating him before the entire group. Jack would have to be a saint in order to ignore Larry and not feel angry toward him for the hurt he has caused. Most likely, Jack will try to get back at Larry in some way. He probably will divert his attention from seeking ways to improve the Olympics to ways for getting even with Larry. Other discussants may well be shuddering inside, wondering if, and even fearing that, Larry will attack them, too. They may be diverting their attention to defenses so as to prevent similar behavior directed at them. Such attacking, aggressive behavior is therefore disruptive to the discussion because it leads people away from their concern with the topic at hand, diverts their concern for the group to personal, defensive behaviors, and thereby creates a negative climate among the group members.

Thwarting Behavior

MARY: I don't understand how the Olympics works. Would you please explain it to me, the part about gold medals and silver, too?

ELAINE: I've said it before—why are we discussing the Olympics anyhow? It's so stupid; here we are talking about the Olympics when we should be looking at something else. Do we *have to* discuss the Olympics?

Elaine doesn't attack any single member; she attacks the entire group. In effect she is saying to the group that it has made a wrong decision to discuss the Olympic games. But, as the remark by Mary indicates, the group is not now discussing *what* should be the topic. The group is already discussing the Olympics itself and Elaine is persisting in her desire to get everyone off the common course of action. The tone of her statement is negative. (You might sense this better if you read Elaine's remark aloud.) The message is one of petulance and disapproval. She is trying to thwart the group from proceeding and doesn't even offer an alternative topic for consideration. Such behavior is disruptive because the group must leave its concern for the Olympics and somehow deal with Elaine's blocking move, even if it is only momentary.

Pleading Own Case

> GERRY (for the third time): I want to return to the role of travel agencies in promoting the Olympics. I remember once that a travel agent told me about their importance especially when . . .

Gerry doesn't attack anyone in particular or the group in general. He just wants to have his say. He's "hung up" on travel agencies and wants to talk about them only. It doesn't matter to him if the group has moved beyond the ways of improving the relationship of the Olympics to travel agencies. He keeps coming back to his pet topic. His small, special interest is of concern to him, and he doesn't care about what is of concern to the group. Such behavior is disruptive to a discussion because it effectively means that one person, such as Gerry, is outside the group and has an ax to grind for himself. At any moment he will enter the flow of interaction to plead his case for his own concern.

It is immediately apparent from these three examples of "disruptive" behavior that a person need not be an outright delinquent, or a discipline case, or even boisterous to disrupt a discussion. Perhaps "negative" behavior would be a better label. In any case, what Larry, Elaine, and Gerry do in the examples above is go against the grain of group discussion and speak in a way that shows that they do not have the progress of the discussion in mind as they talk. They are not concerned with the group or the feelings of the other discussants. Rather, they are concerned at the moment only with themselves. They have very limited vision in that such immediate concern for their individual needs will bring problems, not satisfaction, in the long run. They are hindering, not helping, the discussion.

There are many other types of disruptive behavior. Whether you wish to call such behavior disruptive, or negative, or distracting, or individual rather than group, or even dysfunctional, all of them have the same quality. They all are antigroup discussion in that they hinder the flow of the exchanges between discussants, making things uneasy, shaky, and restricted. They obstruct the discussion flow like a huge bolder does the flow of a rural creek. The list below is an attempt to specify the types of negative behavior.*

1. attacking (being aggressive)
2. blocking
3. competing
4. dominating
5. horsing around
6. inserting irrelevant comments
7. disrupting
8. recognition seeking (boasting; clowning)
9. speaking sarcastically or antagonistically
10. special interest pleading
11. status seeking
12. sympathy seeking
13. taking tangents (drifting)
14. withdrawing (being an outsider, cynical, nonchalant, or indifferent)

It is not necessary to learn this list by heart in order to diagnose a bad situation properly. If your diagnosis indicates trouble, you know that the impeder is not performing as a group member should and that a negative tone is building up in the group. You must take action fast to prevent the destruction of—or at least a serious blow to—your discussion since negative behavior is like a contagious disease spreading through a populous city.

You must take action. At times you yourself as well as others

---

*For material on types of negative behavior see Kenneth D. Benne and Paul Sheats, "Functional Roles of Group Members," *The Journal of Social Issues*, 4, no. 2 (Spring 1948), 41–49; Leland P. Bradford, *Making Meetings Work* (La Jolla, Calif.: University Associates, 1976), pp. 48–49; and William Fawcett Hill, *Learning Thru Discussion*, revised ed. (Beverly Hills, Calif.: Sage Publications, 1969), p. 38.

will view this action as controlling. Indeed, at times it may be so because you are dealing with disruption. Nevertheless, with your eye on the good of the group, you must take action when there is negative behavior. Hopefully, you will not need to do this often nor need to involve the group in chastising someone. Thus, you should try preventive action before the discussion begins; if that doesn't work, preventive action during the discussion; if that does not work, try a "Band-Aid cure"; and, when all else fails, you should try "surgery." In short, it is a four-step procedure.

PREVENTIVE ACTION BEFORE THE DISCUSSION

The absolute best way to deal with negative discussion behavior is prevention. The old adage applies 100 percent to discussions: an ounce of prevention is worth a pound of cure. Let's deal with that ounce before we deal with the pound. We turn our attention now to preventive action before the discussion even begins.

Review Plans before the Discussion

To prevent disruption you must focus on the six discussion leading skills as you carefully plan the discussion and lead it. It is well worth your time, effort, and peace of mind to plan carefully and review your plans *just before the discussion begins*. In light of the specific negative behaviors listed above, ask yourself some questions.

Guideline Questions for Taking Preventive Action
Before *the Discussion*

1. How will I encourage the various people to participate even before the discussion begins?
2. How will I introduce the topic?
3. What is the key question of the discussion—the question whose answer will serve as the cornerstone for describing our achievement during the discussion.

4. In what ways can I myself best contribute but not dominate?
5. Whom shall I sit next to?
6. Where shall I sit?
7. Are there certain discussants who should and shouldn't sit together?
8. How will I support discussants who have in the past been quiet?
9. How can I arrange the chairs so as to convey a positive nonverbal message?
10. What special tasks can I assign people who have been negative in the past (for example, group recorder, greeter, timekeeper, designated first speaker, periodic summarizer)?

The answers to these questions will lead you to critical preventive action, which is as important to a discussion as preventive tooth brushing is to proper dental care. Some of the items below repeat material from the chapter on how to plan a discussion (see Chapter 3). But it is appropriate to state them again here because the importance of preventive action before the discussion even begins cannot be overemphasized. It is a key to successful leadership.

Support Potential Disruptive Discussants

After you review your plans, take time to talk to members who you suspect at this point in time may be disruptive. *Support* them verbally and nonverbally before the discussion. Tell them that you look forward to their unique contributions and thank them ahead of time for their cooperation.

Write Out Introduction

Write out your introduction. Write it out so that you can be sure you have the topic clearly framed in your own mind. Look at your statement to see if there are ways to clarify it; a clear *introducing* of the topic is critical to getting the attention of the discussants and launching the discussion on the right foot.

Review Questions and Facts

Review the key questions to be asked during the discussion. Try to put these questions in some sensible order that yields a strategy and a smooth flow.

Rephrase in your own words and star the key question, subsuming all the rest. Try to answer it yourself so you can be familiar with it and get the feel of it.

Write down some facts you're aware of which are essential; some explanations; and your opinions. Jot down how you think the group should proceed so you can contribute to the group when it is deciding what steps and process to follow.

Assign Discussion Roles

Anticipate who will be present, list their names, and describe to yourself their potential discussion behavior. Suggest some special jobs for those with a potential for negative behavior. Request these people to perform special roles. Decide who could serve as "group memory." Choose a designated first speaker. (The role of the designated first speaker is to speak first after an initial film is seen or story read or field trip taken or question asked.) Choose a person responsible for greeting and seating members as they arrive, especially latecomers. Choose someone to be periodic summarizer. (The role of the periodic summarizer is to summarize from two to four times the main substantive points of the discussion; you or the periodic summarizer can determine when the appropriate times are.) Choose a timekeeper who can keep you on schedule. Don't forget that special roles elicit special behavior, which tends to be positive rather than negative. In assigning discussion roles, attempt to involve as many people in the group as possible and to provide for a person's growth.

Decide on Seating Arrangements

Decide where you will sit and near whom you can sit. Your close presence will influence discussants to act positively. By being able to make eye contact and "smile contact" you can induce people to follow you as leader. Set up the room in a preferred seating arrangement so that easy exchanges between discussants can occur.

In doing these things you will be taking active steps to prevent disruption. You will be setting certain people on a positive path, telling them that you care about their participation. You will be indicating to them what you expect. By being firm and organized you will send clear nonverbal messages with strong impact. Doing such things goes beyond the planning of the substantive, strategic elements of the discussion, which is surely necessary but not sufficient.

Most of all there will be a positive effect on you. Your confidence will improve because you will know that you're prepared and that you've tried your best. Your fear of the worst possible disruption will subside simply because you have faced the issue ahead of time, before the fast and complex interaction begins. It is always easier to deal with such matters when things are simpler, when you can talk with people personally and confidentially. It is always easier to deal with a germ of disruption before the discussion than with a plague of disorder during it.

PREVENTIVE ACTION DURING THE DISCUSSION

In addition to taking preventive action *before* the discussion begins, it is possible and necessary to act *during* the discussion in order to prevent negative behavior. Especially during the early minutes of the discussion you will get messages—primarily nonverbal ones—about the progress and tone of the discussion as well as who might act negatively. For example, if during the early moments a discussant seems angry about the decision to discuss a particular aspect of the broad topic, you should be on the alert to prevent attacking, blocking, or withdrawing by that person.

To help you diagnose the ongoing discussion quickly, ask yourself some questions.

Guideline Questions for Taking Preventive Action
During *the Discussion*

1. What is the social-emotional climate?
2. Are we following the planned discussion?
3. Is the group satisfied with and settled into the topic?
4. Who is and who isn't participating?

Be Clear in Introduction

With prevention in mind take care in your *introduction*. Be clear; be firm; be brief. Make sure everyone is clear as to what the broad topic and specific subtopic are. Check with the discussants by asking them a question:

> LEADER: Is it clear now that we're discussing how we can *improve* the Olympics?
>
> LEADER: We've all decided to look at the future rather than the past in regard to the Olympics. We're zeroing in on *improvement* with everyone's consent. Am I right?

Such moves will help deter blocking and special-interest pleading. This is especially so if you can indicate that the *group* has decided on the topic. It is also necessary to be firm and positive so that the discussants get the message of direction and leadership.

> LEADER: O.K. let's begin our discussion on the Olympics by examining ways to *improve* those important games. Please address yourself to this topic and save others concerned with the Olympics for another time. I know that everyone here knows at least one way to improve the Olympics.
>
> or
>
> LEADER: With your permission, then, we'll begin discussing the topic we've all agreed upon—ways to *improve* the Olympic games. I know that we can generate a bare minimum of ten ways, and I'm eager to hear your suggestions as you demonstrate analysis and imagination. Let's begin our discussion.

With such statements in your *introduction* you aim at encouraging the group and removing any latent doubt about the discussants' desire and ability to discuss the topic. You try to prevent withdrawing, going off on tangents, horsing around, and blocking. You are firm about what the topic is. You also state that the topic has the approval of the group and that the group can successfully respond to the question.

Express Support for the Discussants

After the discussion has begun and a few people have spoken, be sure to express your support for the discussants. Compliment them on the progress they have made via the insightful points they have raised. This will encourage further positive interaction and prevent someone from attempting to go off on a tangent or block the group's progress.

> LEADER: Just a word here on my part to commend you for your incisive responses to the questions so far.
>
> or
>
> LEADER: Your analysis of the Olympics issue is super. Keep it up.

As the discussion moves along, mentally note if a particular person is not participating verbally. Try to involve a nonactive person so as to help the discussion by adding another speaker's viewpoint as well as by preventing that person's withdrawal. Do not force a person to contribute verbally, however, for it is important to remember that listeners are essential to a discussion. Without listeners, speakers can't talk meaningfully.

Prevent Tension Buildup

As the discussion proceeds, you may detect that there is a growing tension in general or between two particular people. You can prevent any further buildup of tension, reduce or eliminate the tension, and avert a crisis in several different ways. First, you can try to involve additional discussants who have a different perspective. With new people speaking and others quiet, there may be a change in mood and the opportunity to calm down.

Break Group into Subgroups. If the situation doesn't improve, then another tactic is to break the group into small groups—even pairs or trios—for a few minutes to work intensively on a particular point. Such a move will reduce the tension by changing the exchanges between discussants. For example, let us use the illustrative discussion on "Fighting Inflation" from Chapters 4 and 5. Let us assume that tension has been building up early. You could enter the discussion in the following way.

> LEADER: We now need to examine some alternatives to saving in a bank. I'd like you to take a few minutes to talk with your neighbors in twos or threes; each pair or trio should try to come up with a list of about five alternatives. Then we'll get together again to put all the suggestions together. O.K., go ahead; we'll get back together in a short while.

By changing the focus and by making the exchanges take place in a more intimate setting, the tone of the discussion will change, too. By the time the group reconvenes as a total unit, much of the tension will most likely be gone.

Change Seating. It is also possible to reduce tension caused by one disruptive person by changing your position relative to that person. You may be able to switch seats during a break or during a small group interlude, as suggested above. Even just standing close to a person will help. Your proximity to a disruptive person is often incentive enough to effect improved behavior. You can also use the opportunity to say some *supporting* words to that person, encouraging and requesting positive behavior in the total group setting.

Along this line it may be advisable to separate two persons if the interaction between them is disruptive. You can pair off discussants briefly for a "consultation session," taking care to break up the disruptive pair. During the interlude you can speak with one or both persons or switch position with one of them.

You can also accomplish a separation smoothly by calling for small groups to meet briefly at various spots in the room. You can then reassemble the group in a new seating arrangement.

Use Humor. You can also prevent a crisis by making the tone lighter through humor. The catch here is not to destroy the serious tone needed for a discussion through too much humor in the attempt to save the discussion. The maxim of taking care not to throw out the baby with the bathwater applies here.

Maintain a Lively Pace

Another tactic to keep in mind for preventing disruption due to boredom is to keep the discussion moving at a lively pace. Rather than stay with one subtopic for a long time, it is helpful to move on to a new subtopic, retaining the option to return if needed or desired. If you sense boredom, then you can move on to a new subtopic with a focusing move. For example, in "Fighting Inflation" you could enter and say:

LEADER: I suggest we leave this point for now. We can come back later to seek other alternatives to bank savings accounts; we have seven alternatives and they're enough to give everyone an idea about what's possible. Let's now address our attention to the element of fear of using these alternatives. Julie, will you expand on the element of being scared since you raised it, and then everyone can comment, too.

With such a comment you can move on and yet not give the discussants the feeling that the floor is closed forever to the listing of additional alternatives to savings accounts in banks. You retain the option to come back to the topic, leaving anyone who feels it necessary to add or seek additional alternatives the possibility of doing so. The discussion moves on, and you prevent stagnation with it concomitant feeling of boredom.

Support Discussants Right to Speak

Negative behavior during a discussion often stems from a person's frustration due to not being permitted to speak. If a discussant cannot enter the discussion after several attempts because of several dominant speakers, that person will soon lose interest. The possibility is great for withdrawal, note-passing to a neighbor, and snide remarks as an undercurrent to the discussion. The same effects are possible from a person who is interrupted by others. Therefore, if the discussants are not monitoring their own behavior, you must explicitly support all discussants who wish to speak. Creating a short waiting list is an excellent tactic for letting everyone know who will speak next and make it easy for less assertive people to enter the interaction.

> LEADER: Several of you want to speak. So, let's have Julie, Jim, George, and Rachel comment in that order.

The key here is to be firm about the order once you've established it. Firmness prevents disruption. Do not let discussants butt in ahead of their turn or enter by interrupting, however innocent the interruption may appear.

> LEADER: George, it's Julie's turn to speak. Your turn comes after Jim, who is next.
>
> or
>
> LEADER: George, please let Julie talk. It's her turn. Julie, continue please.

You must indicate by your verbal and nonverbal support that each person has the right to speak and others have the obligation to listen. You are not only creating order in the present by supporting people but also preventing future disruption. If the discussants need your help, act with firmness.

Assess Substance of Ongoing Discussion

As you keep your one ear, so to speak, on the climate and the dynamics of the ongoing interaction, you must keep your other ear tuned in on the substance of the discussion. Consult your key questions and outline that you have planned ahead of time. If you sense that the discussion is getting off the track, you must

make a judgment: let the discussion head for unchartered terri-
tory or keep it on the planned route. It may, at times, be better to
let the discussion go where the discussants wish to take it. If you
choose to let the discussion leave the planned outline, you
should be aware that you run the risk of making some people
unhappy. Some people will feel deserted or cheated that they
spent their time with something other than the announced topic.
Their unhappiness may lead them to turn negative.

Going off the Track. On the one hand, it requires greater attention on your part to continually assess a new, unexpected situation. It will be more "brain strain" on you to understand what
people are saying, to crystallize their comments as they drift off
topic, to ask critical and appropriate questions, and to draw
conclusions at the closing of the discussion if you move away
from your plans. On the other hand, a discussion that veers from
your outlined path may more truly reflect the needs and desires of
the discussants. Spontaneity has a definitive value for motivation and exploration. You must decide how you will act or react
by considering the advantages and disadvantages.

Staying on the Track. If you do decide to keep the discussion on
your planned track, then you must enter the discussion at an
opportune time to prevent disruptive behavior. After deciding,
wait a bit to see if the discussants bring themselves back to the
original topic. If they do not, then you must act explicitly:

LEADER: Let's please stay with our agreed upon topic of ways to
improve the Olympics. Keep your eyes on improvement, please.

Connected to this matter of keeping on the track is the boredom or frustration of discussants caused by someone who somehow seems to say things slightly or considerably off target. It
seems that the speaker who drifts or says things way out of line
often manages also to be long-winded. For example,

ED: Well, you know about the Olympics. That reminds me of when I
was in Munich last year. Now that's only a few years after the

1972 Olympics. I was talking to this American who's been living there for twenty years. Well, he said that the town felt the impact of the murders by those Arab terrorists . . .

Your task here is to prevent Ed from drifting and causing others to be bored by his remarks. You have a double matter on your hands. You can deal with both matters by listening for the opportune moment to enter the discussion to ask Ed a question concerning the relevancy of his remarks to the subtopic at hand. Ed may not even realize he's drifting or that he's boring others. He had a marvelous time in Munich and wants to share it with others by recounting some of his experiences. He has a point in mind, but he's not able to get to it or make it clear. So, you enter:

LEADER: Ed, would you tell us how this specifically relates to improving the current Olympic games?

Your question of relevance will guide Ed back to the topic. You've gently told him that you don't understand his point but want to, and he may not even realize that. He probably is thankful that you've rescued him from himself because he doesn't intend to be disruptive or unclear. He may come back with a statement like this:

ED: Well, my point is about security. If we improve the security, the whole tone of friendly games among athletes of the world will improve, you see. That's all—better security.

If, however, Ed doesn't make himself clear and brief even after your question, you can take slightly stronger action. You can remind him that time is limited, that three other people are waiting to speak after him, or that you still don't see his point. Or, you can send nonverbal messages that you are eager yourself to say something (a crystallizing move). Or, by nodding to another person you can show that someone else is eager to speak. The point is that you must prevent Ed from acting negatively even if he does so unconsciously and with good will. Remember to thank Ed for his point once he's made it clear.

APPLYING A "BAND-AID CURE"

Although prevention is the best way to deal with negative behavior, it is not always possible to succeed in avoiding serious trouble. There are times when you must take action to solve a problem caused by disruption. You may, of course, have to purchase your solution at a dear price because you may need a pound of cure where an ounce of prevention would have worked five or ten minutes earlier. Sometimes you may not even be able to find a solution other than adjournment.

Take Action

In preventive action and statements you do not explicitly acknowledge trouble. You take action subtly to prevent negative behavior before it arises. Thus, you try not to alert the discussants to disruption because their attention to the substance of the discussion will suffer if you do. When you take steps to treat the problem with the group, you do call attention to the problem and thereby run the risk of magnifying it as well as solving it.

Indicate Desired Behavior

The preferred action, therefore, is for you to always try prevention first. But if prevention does not work, then you should try a "Band-Aid" solution. Hopefully, a Band-Aid solution will suffice and eliminate the need for an operation under anesthesia. Always try the Band-Aid cure before rushing into an operation. Confront the problem delicately:

> LEADER: George, you're interrupting. Please do not interrupt. Let Julie speak.
>
> or
>
> LEADER: Jim, you've been quiet and out of it so far. May we hear from you now or very soon.
>
> or
>
> LEADER: We're drifting away from our agreed upon topic. No drifting, please. Stay on the topic.

Note that here you do alert the discussants to the problem by identifying it. In the three examples above you use the words "interrupting," "quiet and out of it," and "drifting." You do not make a big fuss, however. Rather, you state briefly what the problem is and briefly what the desired behavior is. It is important to follow the negative with the positive. Such Band-Aid action is often enough to curtail disruption, even when someone mutters barbed remarks to a neighbor about what's going on.

Thus, there are three key elements in this Band-Aid cure:

1. Briefly note that there is trouble.
2. Briefly indicate the desired behavior.
3. Focus on behavior rather than personality.

Focus on Behavior

Let us examine the third element, since we have already looked at the first two. The third element is subtle but cannot be overemphasized. Compare these two remarks:

LEADER: George, you're interrupting. Please do not interrupt.
LEADER: George, you are an interrupter. Don't be an interrupter.

Whereas in the first remark you are focusing on what George is doing at the moment, in the second one you are focusing on George's personality. It is easier for George to cope with his present behavior because he can probably alter it than with his personality. His behavior may be a function of his enthusiasm about the topic. But it is much more difficult for George to cope with his personality, for he cannot change it easily or quickly. His personality is a function of years of development.

It is absolutely essential for these reasons that you avoid calling George an interrupter. *Identify the behavior; do not label the personality.* George and everyone else will agree that George has interrupted. But George in particular and others as well may not agree that George is an interrupter. George, as interrupter, may become quite defensive, then argumentative, and thus seriously disruptive. A slight change in phrasing thus yields a significant difference. There is no doubt that "personal labeling only increases individual defensiveness."†

Sometimes it will be helpful for you to *point out the effects of the negative behavior* because the discussants may not be aware of it. You may thus be helping them become self-aware and better able to change to positive behavior.

> LEADER: Jim, you've been quiet and out of it so far. We haven't heard about the Olympics from your particular vantage point as a sportscaster. Your comments would help, I believe. May we hear from you now or very soon.

Note the difference here between this "cure" and the previous one directed to Jim. The insertion of the two middle sentences gives the effect of Jim's withdrawal and it softens the remarks. Once Jim and the other discussants recognize the loss suffered because Jim has been quiet, the probability increases that Jim will improve. He probably will offer comments, and the others may ask him specific comments to correct the noted deficiency.

SEEKING STRONG ACTION FOR A
MAJOR DISRUPTION: SURGERY

If your attempt at a Band-Aid cure doesn't succeed, then you will have to try a stronger action to eliminate negative behavior. You will have to try surgery to solve the problem. For example, you sense that several people are antagonistic toward the topic, toward you, and toward the other discussants. No matter what you've tried, the discussion is not progressing. Furthermore, you sense that others, too, feel a negative tone in the room. Here you must confront the problem. But here you will not be as subtle or delicate as before. Here you present the behavior problem to the group for them to cope with, since it is not your problem alone as leader but *everyone's problem*.

---

†Bradford, *Making Meetings* Work, p. 50.

Seek Group Solution

LEADER: I think it's time we all take a serious look at what's going on here. I sense a feeling of anger in the group. Fifteen minutes have already passed and we have not answered the first question yet. People are cutting off others while talking; some people are muttering under their breath to their neighbors; and some people have not participated yet at all. We have a problem here that we must look at and solve together because we are now hindering ourselves. What shall we do to improve this situation so we can proceed with our discussion?

With such a statement you deliberately and directly present the problem to the group for them to solve. You make no bones about it being a problem and that it's everyone's problem. The disrupters and those who allow them to disrupt must together seek a solution. If Sam, for example, is disruptive by clowning and interrupting, then it's not your problem alone, or Sam's problem alone, but everyone's problem. Encourage the group to deal with Sam about his behavior. Let them indicate that they are unhappy with his clowning and interrupting. Do not become the spokesperson of the group or their police officer because they are too shy or afraid of Sam. The negative behavior is everyone's problem.

Focus on Behavior. Once again, in your statement and question requesting a solution, refer to the behavior of the discussants and not their personalities, for it is their behavior that you're asking them to change. Your question asks the group to give suggestions for improvement in *behavior*. The question is "What shall WE DO? with emphasis on the "we" and "do."

Analyze What's Happening. In effect, you have stopped the discussion in order for everyone to take a step back from it in order to analyze what's happening. Since you have decided to take a major step, you have very little to lose in that the discussion has been poor anyhow. The group must now cope with itself or quit because it isn't functioning adequately as a group in any case. It is time for everyone to look at the dynamics of the group rather then to continue their substantive exchanges.

Seek Suggestions for the Future. It is important that you lead the group to look at what it is doing now and what it will do in the future. There is not much point in examining the past in order to seek explanations. Most people simply won't or even can't explain why they behave as they do. Or, they may not be ready to be 100 percent honest and frank with each other. But they can and must agree on positive, courteous behavior so that a group discussion can take place.

Therefore, if some people begin to ask for explanations of causes, try to shift them to suggestions for future action. Ask people to agree upon several rules and ways to proceed. For example,

1. No interrupting
2. Speak only when called on by the leader for the next 10 minutes or so until we get back on the track
3. Work in subgroups for a short while (10 to 15 minutes) so as to get a fresh start
4. Everyone change seats; "scramble the basket"
5. Rearrange the seats
6. Each speaker limited to one minute at a time
7. Each person pledges to help the group
8. Select a new topic
9. Take a short break

Rearrange Seating

Since it is difficult to correct a bad situation by only speaking differently, it is best to take the opportunity for a fresh start by changing the physical environment, too. That is, rearrange the seats, if possible, to facilitate a new set of neighbors and exchanges.

Work in Subgroups

An excellent—perhaps the very best—tactic in starting anew is to work in subgroups on a specific point. This will provide (1) new groupings among discussants; (2) easy and more intimate exchanges that help get over the unpleasantness of confronting a bad situation; and (3) lots of fresh ideas to kick off the whole group discussion once you reconvene. Getting going as a whole group again will be easy, since you will have people ready to contribute the ideas from their subgroups. Remember to circulate among the small groups while they meet so you can reestablish contact with everyone.

Confronting the problem with the group in an attempt to solve it can work if there is a commitment to a group procedure and group interest. If people care for each other and trust each other, then they can gain by examining their own negative behavior and finding a way of improving it. If there has been an attempt in the past to develop positive behavior and you have demonstrated appropriate support previously, then a short detour can help the group. The group solution can become its own positive element in furthering the future development of the group.

Your Intervention May Be Necessary

Though you may ask the group to solve its problem, there are times, however, where the group will ask you as leader to offer suggestions for solving a serious problem it has. You certainly can and should contribute suggestions. But you must take care to do so only after others have begun. Under no circumstance ought you to be the only one to offer suggestions or take the burden of responsibility for solving the problem yourself. After all, it is the group's problem and not yours alone. Unless the group is willing to participate in solving the problem and thereby declare its good intentions and sense of "ownership" of the solution, the proposed solution has little chance of succeeding.

If you have tried preventing negative behavior to no avail and tried curing a bad situation once it has arrived also to no avail, then you might be best off asking for adjournment. This is indeed an appropriate course to follow when you feel that the prospects for correction are virtually hopeless. You should remember that you need not lead any discussion under duress. It may just be better to cut the loss rather than continue to compound trouble. Simply ask the group to disband rather than continue to create further trouble.

Thus, there are six key points to keep in mind as you confront a major problem with the group and seek a solution to the negative behavior.

Guidelines for Taking Strong Action to Solve a Major Disruption

1. Briefly note that there is trouble.
2. Focus on behavior rather than personality.
3. Indicate that it is a *group* problem.
4. Request the entire group to suggest corrective action.
5. Go beyond words and implement physical changes as well so as to effect a fresh start.
6. Be willing to disband completely.

7

DISCUSSION FEEDBACK
AND EVALUATION

Do you remember what you did after you bought your car, sofa, or stereo set? Do you remember what you did after returning from your vacation? Most likely you talked about your purchase or vacation. It's normal and necessary to do so. Just as you needed to think alone and talk with others as you planned your vacation in the first place, so, too, you needed to think alone and talk with other people about your vacation after you came home. Planning is needed before an action, and reflection is needed after it.

After you lead a discussion, you need to consider how it went. You need to ask yourself some questions, such as: What did I do? How did the various participants perform? How do the participants perceive what happened? Do the participants perceive my leadership as effective? How can the discussants and I improve? What would I do differently if I were to repeat the discussion? What would I do the same if I were to repeat the discussion? What do I like best and least about the discussion? Was the discussion outstanding? Was it poor? Was it somewhere between outstanding and poor? There is almost an infinite number of specific questions you can ask, but in short, you want to know what happened, how effective the discussion and your leadership were, and what you can do to improve as a discussion leader. (You need to ask about improvement because everyone can always improve; there's no such person as the perfect discussion leader for all times.)

There are several broad actions that you must perform in order to answer these questions—the actions of giving feedback to others, giving feedback to yourself, soliciting feedback from others, receiving feedback from others, and evaluating your discussion leadership. Let us treat each one of these actions specifically in order.

GIVING FEEDBACK TO OTHERS

It is often appropriate to give feedback to the other discussants in terms of your perception of how they performed during the discussion. This occurs when you are a teacher or group leader leading a discussion with your class, club, or committee. One of your goals may be to speak with the group as a whole afterwards or with individual discussants separately.

Purpose of Feedback

The purpose of giving feedback to another person is to help that person maintain good behavior and improve behavior by knowing more about what's happened or at least knowing what's happened from another vantage point. Thus, feedback is not the same as evaluation, since feedback provides *information* to a person rather than a *value judgment* of that person. The underlying notion of feedback is that people can and will do their own evaluation of a situation and seek to improve. They will change because they have a desire and motivation to do well, and their impetus to change is the dissonance they feel has been created by the information they receive. This dissonance is the tension they feel between what happened and what they would like to have happened. To remove the dissonance they will change their behavior in the future to bring it closer to the preferred behavior they have chosen.

Focus on Behavior

With feedback you focus on the person's behavior—what that person did and how it affects others—rather than on what you feel that person is or on how you judge that person. Feedback is therefore less threatening to the receiver, and thus the person is more willing to accept the message received. With feedback you must rely on the other person's motivation, the ability to draw her or his own conclusions, and the ability to set a personal path to improvement or at least to seek help in order to improve. This may appear to be too much for you to allow the other person. Yet, this approach to improvement is entirely consistent with the very concepts of discussion and discussion leadership presented earlier. That is, people deserve respect for their abilities, and they cherish their independence for thought and action. They are responsible for their behavior in a mutually helping atmosphere.

An emphasis on evaluating people and telling them how to improve runs counter to the entire approach to discussion presented here. Few of us, if any, enjoy having other people evaluate us. We may beam when we hear positive points, but we flinch and even hurt when someone tells us we performed poorly—when we deserve a "D" grade or worse. Although the giving of "gold stars" may at times motivate people to improve, the reliance on external evaluation from others serves to create a sense of dependence rather than independence. If you encourage the "gold star" approach, you must also accept the flip side of the external coin—the "you failed" evaluations that are contrary to self-growth because they devastate and anger the evaluated person.

It is also true that, given our society, it is impossible for us to be nonevaluative. We all make evaluations of others at one time or another. Some we make explicitly and some implicitly by the way we act or by the choice of behavior we focus on. Though we may try to be nonevaluative by giving feedback rather than evaluations and directions, we may not completely succeed. Nor is some evaluation, especially with younger people who are developing their sense of independence, entirely inappropriate. Young people look to adult leaders who are their models for guidance and approval, even correction, as they move toward independence.

In short, an emphasis on evaluation of other discussants is to be avoided in favor of the giving of feedback that relies on *self-evaluation*. (Indeed, in the long run, even an external evaluation is effective only when a person accepts that evaluation as his or her own.) Feedback that signifies a sense of respect for independent thought is preferable because it fosters the growth of independence and avoids threat as it paves the way for a person to improve. Feedback informs a person about what happened and allows a person to deal with that information in a personal way, most likely in a way that will lead to improvement for self-benefit and group benefit.

To give feedback in a helpful way and to avoid evaluation as much as possible requires sensitivity to the other discussant, knowledge of the interactions during the discussion, and skill based on practice. You also need some basic rules about giving feedback.

Five Basic Rules for Giving Feedback

1. You must make clear to the receiver that your intention is to help bring about improvement, and that your intention is not humiliation, evaluation, or one-upmanship. Remember, feedback is helpful when trust exists between the people involved.
2. You must make clear what is considered appropriate or good discussion behavior, thus establishing standards or characteristics. You can use the characteristics of a discussion as presented in the answer in Chapter 2 to the question, "What Is a Discussion?" Or, you can use the items listed in the Self-Survey of Discussion Leadership.
3. You must alert the receiver to the dissonance between what is desired and what happened if you wish to provide the motivation for change.
4. You must indicate that this change involves low risk or else the discussant will shy away from an attempt at it.
5. Most important, you must provide support for change by

being a model of good discussion behavior and by praising change when it occurs.

To aid you in abiding by these rules so that you can give useful feedback, some guidelines follow.

Guidelines for Giving Helpful, Meaningful Feedback to a Discussant

1. *Focus feedback on the actual performance of the discussant rather than on the discussant's personality.* Comment on what the discussant did or said during the discussion and the effect it had. For example, speak about the question asked that was a turning point in the discussion or the effect the remarks had on a third person, or the effect of sitting outside the group and not saying one word for the first two-thirds of the discussion, or the support the discussant gave others by listening attentively and aptly recapitulating their remarks. Such comments are preferable to speaking about the discussant as a charming person, dominating person, disruptive influence, or a person on an "ego trip."

2. *Focus feedback on observations rather than assumptions or inferences.* It is important to focus on what you heard and saw rather than on what you assume went on, or what you infer is the motivation behind the behavior, or how you explain what happened. The observations you use should be your own rather than those reported to you by someone else. For example, comment that you saw the discussant passing notes to a neighbor the entire time, or that the discussant only asked questions and then only to one specific person, or that as a person filling the role of "greeter and seater" the discussant failed to welcome the two new people from the visiting class. Do not offer such comments as: "From the way you spoke to Joe you probably had an argument with him before the discussion"; or "I'm sure you raised your voice and shouted because you were once in a similar spot as captain of your tennis team"; or "You asked those questions because your mother is a lawyer." If you feel that you must get at an explanation, then by all means phrase your remarks as a question the discussant can respond to. For example, "Did you

shout at Mary because of your loss to her in the countywide tennis tournament?''

3. *Focus feedback on description rather than evaluation.* Keep in mind that the purpose of feedback is to inform the discussant about what happened and what effects her or his behavior had during the discussion. To achieve this purpose you should focus on describing behavior rather than evaluating it. Talk about *what* rather than *how well*. For example, you might say, ''You didn't participate verbally until the last ten minutes of the discussion'' rather than ''It's a bad policy for you to sit back and just listen to others until just before the end of the discussion.'' Or you might say, ''When you participated by reacting to Joe's comment on the phoniness of the Olympics, Mary and Jane spoke for the first time, too.''

4. *Focus feedback on the specific and concrete rather than the general and abstract.* Talk about the specific and concrete so that the discussant can interpret or generalize on his or her own. The discussant can handle the specific more easily than a generalization formed by you. Just as an evaluation has meaning if it is a self-evaluation, so too does a generalization formulated personally by the discussant become meaningful. It is better for you not to impose a pattern or interpretation that may threaten the discussant because it may imply a noncorrectable trend. For example, you can comment that the discussant asked Joe three questions or that the discussant was wrong regarding the location of the 1968 summer Olympics. Such statements are preferable to ''You seem to like to ask boys questions'' or ''You're not able somehow to get your facts correct when you talk about sports.''

5. *Focus feedback on the present rather than on the past.* It is important to give feedback to the discussants when the discussion is fresh and still in their minds. Then it is possible to remember the events that occurred as well as their sequence. When the discussion is fresh in their minds, they can make connections and plan action that will lead to desired changes or improvement. The context of time and place, which accompanies feedback in the present, helps make the feedback meaningful. Though in general it is better to give feedback sooner rather than later, there are times when you will have to postpone

giving feedback because of your emotional state or the discussants'. It is important, therefore, for you to be sensitive to the timing of giving your feedback.

6. *Focus feedback on sharing of information rather than on giving advice.* If you create an atmosphere of sharing, that you wish to offer what you know to the discussant for consideration together, then you create a nonthreatening situation. If the information is *shared* information, the discussant is free to use it in whatever ways seem most appropriate. If you give *advice*, on the other hand, you are evaluating and telling the discussant what to do. This sets up a threatening situation since you show yourself to be superior. You remove the discussant's freedom of choice of action. For example, speak about "perhaps we can sit down together for a few minutes to talk about what happened during the discussion" or "I took some notes during the discussion which I'd like to share with you." Such statements are preferable to "I suggest that you improve your participation by listening more carefully, especially when the speaker is reacting to a previous comment of yours."

7. *Focus feedback on alternatives rather than "the" one best path.* When you focus on alternatives, you open up possible doors and thereby increase freedom of action. The discussant is able and free to choose from what appears best from what is available. This maintains self-respect and independence. When you speak about "the" one best path, you restrict the discussant's freedom. For example, speak about "the possibility of becoming a periodic summarizer, or the designated first speaker, or a presenter" rather than "the best way for you to increase your participation is to become the designated first speaker."

8. *Focus feedback on information and ideas phrased in terms of "more or less" rather than "either/or."* "More or less" terminology shows that there is a continuum along which the discussant's actions fall. "Either/or" terminology suggests an absolute situation of two extremes without any middle ground, without any gray area between the two poles. More or less terminology is more appropriate to discussions, since there are very few, if any, situations with absolute positions. The many complex variables in a discussion require us to keep a sliding continuum in mind without having a predetermined extreme position. For

example, speak about "reacting less often to speakers" or "you crystallized other members' statements more this time than last and the effect was to have these people react favorably to your own remarks." Such statements are preferable to "they accepted you or rejected you, depending on your own position toward them."

9. *Focus feedback on what the discussant (the receiver) needs rather than on what you (the sender) need to get off your chest.* Since the purpose of feedback is to alert the discussant about what happened, you must keep the receiver in mind. Even though you may have several items in mind, not all of them may be appropriate given the circumstance before you. You may get a sense of relief by saying what's on your mind, but the cost may be too high for the discussant. Say less than what's on your mind because you can usually add more later. Feedback and not personal release is what you should aim for as you seek to help the discussant.

10. *Focus feedback on what the discussant can use and manage rather than on all the information you have gathered.* Though you may have taken many written and mental notes during the discussion, you must strive to resist the temptation to overwhelm the discussant with your data. You will destroy the purpose of feedback if your overload the discussant because you will foster a sense of hopelessness or helplessness. If you keep the amount of feedback low, then the receiver can manage to deal with it and seek to improve. Thus, talk about one or two key items rather than eight or nine.

11. *Focus feedback on modifiable items rather than on what the discussant cannot do anything about.* This guideline is obvious but important and unfortunately sometimes overlooked. There is no value to the discussant in focusing on behavior that cannot be changed. The discussant, when confronted by a non-modifiable matter, will feel that there is no hope. On the other hand, by speaking about what can be changed, you encourage the discussant and offer the opportunity to improve. For example, speak about "possibly changing your seat in order to hear better" rather than "your poor hearing keeps you from participating as much as you need to."

12. *Focus feedback on what the discussant requests from you*

rather than on what you could impose. It is advantageous for you to respond to requests of the discussant. Such requests tell you what concerns the discussant. You are in a good position to help in the future with items *you* think are important if you can help the discussant with the immediate, self-selected areas. You can get to these concerns by asking the discussant to identify them. For example, "Is there any area in particular that you'd like me to comment on?" or "Ask me some questions, so I'll know what you're interested in."

13. *Check the feedback you give by asking the discussant to summarize the main points for both of you.* An excellent technique is to ask the person to summarize the main ideas that you two have raised. You will then have a good way to understand how the discussant perceives the situation and how well you have followed the previous twelve guidelines. We often check what we say on the telephone by asking the other person to repeat an address or order number we have given. Such a check often reveals errors in our communication. Similarly, you can benefit by checking the feedback you have given to the discussant.

GIVING FEEDBACK TO YOURSELF

After the discussion you need to think about what happened regarding your own leadership role. This is not an easy matter because human beings have the uncanny ability to hide from asking and answering their own questions. To help remedy this situation it may be necessary to employ a structure that requires you to face the situation. With this in mind, the first thing for you to do is to review what happened by following the above Guidelines for Giving Helpful, Meaningful Feedback to a Discussant. That is, think through the discussion by yourself, focusing on performance rather than personality, observations rather than assumptions, description rather than evaluation and so forth. You can do this alone or with someone else. Often, it helps to have someone to talk to about the discussion, even if this person was not present at the discussion. Just talking it over with someone else is a help.

In addition to such a review, two forms will provide you with a vehicle for examining the discussion. The form, Were I To Lead This Discussion Again, asks you to react to twelve specific items in terms of what you would do differently or the same next time. As you check off your reaction to each item, be sure to fill in the column marked "Notes on Specifics" with either what you would change to effect improvement or what specifically about that item leads you to want to keep it the same.

Were I To Lead This Discussion Again

Discussion Title: _____ Date: _____ Time: _____

	Different	Same	Notes on Specifics
1. Assigned roles (e.g., presenter, periodic summarizer, greeter and seater, recorder, timekeeper, designated first speaker, resource person, final recapitulator, launcher for future, and logician)			
2. Audiovisual aids			
3. Guests			
4. Key questions in discussion strategy			
5. My personal participation			
6. Outline of topic			
7. Participants			
8. Room			
9. Seating arrangement			
10. Specific focus of discussion			
11. Time			
12. Type of discussion (policy, problem solving, explaining, predicting, debriefing)			
13. Other			

The Post-Discussion Self-Rating form offers you fifteen items to respond to as a way of thinking about the discussion. The main section of this form deals with your own perception of how you performed the six discussion skills of contributing, crystallizing, focusing, introducing/closing, questioning, and supporting. You will also find an item concerning your preparation, your avoidance of negative behavior, and your own learning as a result of the discussion. After you have responded to these fifteen items, you can jot down some comments showing what led you to circle the rating number as you did.

Please carefully note the item on learning (Item #13), "I learned something on the topic: new information, insights, and understanding." The scoring of this item shows that it is a good characteristic for you to learn something as discussion leader. If you learn nothing or very little, it is a sign that perhaps there wasn't a "discussion" at all in which you exchanged ideas with the other discussants. Furthermore, if you learned little or nothing, then you should reconsider what discussion skills you performed as well as the attitudes you manifested nonverbally during the discussion. Perhaps your only role was to ask questions as an outsider or as an uninvolved interrogator might. Or, perhaps you only introduced the topic and remained otherwise uninvolved.

SOLICITING FEEDBACK

It is also necessary for you to solicit feedback from others so you can get information from their points of view. For the same reason that you give feedback to the discussants in order to help them improve, so it is necessary for you yourself to receive feedback. However, since you are taking a leadership role you cannot wait for others to voluntarily and spontaneously give you that feedback. You need to solicit feedback or the chances are great that you will not receive it.

In addition to the Guidelines for Soliciting Helpful, Meaningful Feedback for Yourself from a Discussant on page 120, there are three forms for you to use. You may use any one, any two, or all three forms depending on your assessment of the situation.

Post-Discussion Self-Rating

Discussion Title: _____ Date: _____ Time: _____

Please circle the appropriate number from 7 to 1 to indicate your reaction to each item.	High Good Yes Positive	Low Bad No Negative

1. My preparation 7 6 5 4 3 2 1
2. My contribution of facts and
   explanations 7 6 5 4 3 2 1
3. My contribution of personal opinions
   and justifications 7 6 5 4 3 2 1
4. My crystallizing key substantive points 7 6 5 4 3 2 1
5. My crystallizing points regarding the
   tone of the discussion 7 6 5 4 3 2 1
6. My efforts to keep the discussion
   focused 7 6 5 4 3 2 1
7. My introducing of the discussion 7 6 5 4 3 2 1
8. My closing of the discussion 7 6 5 4 3 2 1
9. My questions during the discussion 7 6 5 4 3 2 1
10. My *verbal* support and encouragement
    of group members to participate 7 6 5 4 3 2 1
11. My *nonverbal* support and
    encouragement of group members to
    participate 7 6 5 4 3 2 1
12. My avoidance of negative behaviors
    such as sarcasm, interrupting, and
    domination 7 6 5 4 3 2 1
13. I learned something on the topic: new
    information, insights, and understanding 7 6 5 4 3 2 1
14. My efforts in general 7 6 5 4 3 2 1
15. The overall quality of this discussion 7 6 5 4 3 2 1

The first form, Post-Discussion Reaction, gives you an open-ended look at the discussion. It asks the discussant to rate the discussion in general and then to specify in self-chosen areas and words what was "liked best" and "liked least." It also requests suggestions for improvement. The key here is the open-endedness of the form, allowing the discussant to determine personally and individually what and how to comment. You don't determine the areas for the discussant.

Post-Discussion Reaction

Discussion Title: _____ Date: _____ Time: _____

1. OVERALL I think that this discussion was (circle the appropriate number from 7 to 1)

   outstanding   7 6 5 4 3 2 1   poor

2. The things I LIKED BEST about this discussion are:

3. The things I LIKED LEAST about this discussion are:

4. To IMPROVE the next discussion I suggest:

The second form, Post-Discussion Reaction to Group Climate,* gives you feedback on how the discussant feels about the discussion in regard to the aspects of pleasantness, security, cohesion, purposefulness, objectivity, involvement, cooperativeness, communicativeness, permissiveness, and flexibility.

---

*Based on a similar form in *Discussion in Small Groups: A Guide to Effective Practice*, Third Edition, by David Potter and Martin P. Andersen (Belmont, California: Wadsworth Publishing, Company, Inc., 1976), pp. 115-16.

From this feedback you can make plans to improve your efforts where necessary. For example, if you get low scores on Item #4, Democracy, indicating that you are not permitting the group to make its own decisions, then you might well plan to adjust your own actions to become more of a group-centered leader.

Post-Discussion Reaction to Group Climate

Discussion Title: _____ Date: _____ Time: _____

Please circle the appropriate number from 7 to 1 to indicate your reaction to each item.	High	Low

1. Cohesion: members support one another, stick up for the group, resist outside disruptive forces. 7 6 5 4 3 2 1
2. Communicativeness: remarks seem addressed to everyone; no communication cliques develop; leader does not talk only to a few. 7 6 5 4 3 2 1
3. Cooperativeness: members contribute to the best of their ability; there is little fighting for status and personal goals. 7 6 5 4 3 2 1
4. Democracy: members and leader are group-centered; group makes most decisions; atmosphere relaxed and accepting. 7 6 5 4 3 2 1
5. Flexibility: group adjusts to changing needs, profits from mistakes. 7 6 5 4 3 2 1
6. Involvement: members are eager to participate and do so. 7 6 5 4 3 2 1
7. Objectivity: members are critical of prejudice and avoid it; they seek the best solutions to a problem. 7 6 5 4 3 2 1
8. Pleasantness: everyone seems to enjoy the discussion. 7 6 5 4 3 2 1
9. Purposefulness: goals are understood at start and kept in mind throughout. 7 6 5 4 3 2 1
10. Security: members feel safe in speaking; neither ideas nor people are ridiculed. 7 6 5 4 3 2 1

The third form, Post-Discussion Reaction to the Discussion Leader, gives you feedback mainly on your performance of discussion skills. This form is similar to the Post-Discussion Self-Rating on page 117. After you receive this feedback, you should refer to your own sheet to see how your reactions compare with the discussant's. If the reactions differ widely, then you need to confer personally with the discussant to determine the reasons for the discrepancy in reactions.

Whether or not you confer personally with a discussant because of a discrepancy in reaction to the discussion, you can and should solicit feedback orally according to the guidelines that follow. These guidelines are parallel to the previous set of guidelines, and therefore they are brief.

Guidelines for Soliciting Helpful, Meaningful Feedback for Yourself from a Discussant

1. *Focus feedback on your actual performance rather than on your personality.* Ask the discussant to comment on what you said or did during the discussion. For example, you might say, "I'd like to get some feedback from you about the discussion, specifically on some things I did. Did the questions I asked have the effect of stimulating you to think through the topic carefully?"

2. *Focus feedback on observations rather than assumptions or inferences.* Ask the discussant to comment based on what was actually seen and heard rather than on what was assumed to be happening. For example, you might say, "Based on what you observed, comment on the seating arrangement."

3. *Focus feedback on description rather than evaluation.* It's important for you to learn what happened from another vantage point and to find out about things you didn't hear or see. You might say, "Tell me, as a person sitting at the back of the room, what was the effect of seating Joe to my immediate right?"

4. *Focus feedback on the specific and concrete rather than the general and abstract.* It is better for your future plans for improvement to receive specific comments on items so you can draw conclusions and discover any developing patterns on your

Post-Discussion Reaction to the Discussion Leader

Discussion Title: _____ Date: _____ Time: _____

Please circle the appropriate number from 7 to 1 to indicate your reaction to each item.	High Good Yes Positive				Low Bad No Negative

1. The leader's preparation

    7 6 5 4 3 2 1

2. The leader's contribution of facts and explanations

    7 6 5 4 3 2 1

3. The leader's contribution of personal opinions and justifications

    7 6 5 4 3 2 1

4. The leader's crystallizing (summarizing) key substantive points

    7 6 5 4 3 2 1

5. The leader's crystallizing (summarizing) points regarding the tone of the discussion

    7 6 5 4 3 2 1

6. The leader's efforts to keep the discussion focused

    7 6 5 4 3 2 1

7. The leader's introducing of the discussion

    7 6 5 4 3 2 1

8. The leader's closing of the discussion

    7 6 5 4 3 2 1

9. The leader's questions during the discussion

    7 6 5 4 3 2 1

10. The leader's *verbal* support and encouragement of group members to participate

    7 6 5 4 3 2 1

11. The leader's *nonverbal* support and encouragement of group members to participate

    7 6 5 4 3 2 1

12. The leader's avoidance of negative behaviors such as sarcasm, interrupting, and domination

    7 6 5 4 3 2 1

13. The leader learned something on the topic: new information, insights, and understanding

    7 6 5 4 3 2 1

14. The leader's efforts in general

    7 6 5 4 3 2 1

15. The overall quality of this discussion

    7 6 5 4 3 2 1

own. You might say, "Tell me specifically about the way I introduced the topic. That is, was I brief and clear?"

5. *Focus feedback on the present rather than the past.* Solicit feedback soon after the discussion so that it is possible to still have a fresh and vivid recollection of what happened. Don't worry about the discussion you led two months ago but solicit comments on the one just completed.

6. *Focus feedback on sharing of information rather than on getting advice.* Since it is impossible for you to know everything that occurred during the discussion, you need to ask others to help fill in the gaps of your knowledge. Try to create a sense of pooling of information. Ask the discussant to share knowledge of what happened with you so you can better grasp the effects of your behavior.

7. *Focus feedback on alternatives rather than "the" one best path.* By soliciting alternatives you open up possibilities for yourself as well as nonverbally stating that there is no one best way for everybody, even though some people may think that they have the one best answer. You might say, "Can you offer me two or three suggestions of possible ways to prevent the clowning around by some people?"

8. *Focus feedback on information and ideas phrased in terms of "more or less" rather than "either/or."* When you use more or less terminology, you indicate that there are varying degrees in most matters rather than a dichotomy where there is no gray between the light and dark poles. You might say, "Did I personally contribute more or less than what you expected or desired of me?"

9. *Focus feedback on what you (the leader and receiver) need rather than on what the discussant needs to get off his or her chest.* Keep in mind that the purpose of the feedback is to help you improve in the future or maintain behavior already demonstrated. This need not be the opportunity for the discussant to launch into a long gripe session or admiration session.

10. *Focus feedback on what you can use and manage rather than on all the information the discussant has for you.* The purpose of feedback is to provide you with information you can act on. If you get too much you may feel overwhelmed and thus unable to effect changes at all. After you have some feedback that you consider manageable, you might say, "Thanks for the

feedback; that's about all I can handle right now; perhaps another time you can give me some more ideas to consider."

11. *Focus feedback on modifiable items rather than on what you cannot do anything about.* If you had and will have in the future no control over the location of the discussion room, for example, there is little value in seeking feedback on this point. Focus feedback on items you can determine such as your questions or who served as designated first speaker. Since you are responsible for these items, you particularly need to know the effects of your determinations.

12. *Focus feedback on what the discussant requests to give you rather than on what you could demand from her or him.* Often you will find a discussant who is eager to provide feedback. Either the discussant approaches you to give feedback or begins to specify items once you open the general idea of giving feedback to you. If the discussant has some pressing information to share with you, then by all means solicit it and listen to it.

In short, as you frame your questions to solicit feedback, follow the guidelines. This will direct the discussant to give you feedback, which indeed is consistent with these guidelines, even though the discussant may not be familiar with them.

RECEIVING FEEDBACK

An important supplement to soliciting feedback appropriately is receiving feedback in a meaningful way. If you solicit feedback sincerely, then you must receive it sincerely or the sender will be led to conclude that you really do not want it. If you do not receive feedback in a positive way, then your future solicitations for feedback will not yield you any response. For example, if you ask a discussant to tell you if your questions achieved their purpose of focusing on the topic and you get noticeably angry when you hear the answer, then certainly that person will be most cautious regarding future responses. When that happens, you no longer will receive the feedback you need in order to improve your discussion leadership.

To aid you in receiving feedback in an appropriate way, some guidelines follow.

Guidelines for Receiving Feedback in a Helpful, Meaningful Way

1. *Focus on what is being said rather than on how it is said.* The sender may be shy, angry, or both, and the delivery may bother you somewhat. Nevertheless, you need to hear *what* is said and must therefore discount how the feedback is delivered in order to profit from the feedback.

2. *Focus on feedback as a learning tool rather than as a criticizing one.* Think of the feedback you receive as an opportunity for you to learn about your performance from another vantage point. Do not go on the defensive and consider yourself to be under attack. Keep your head up! Consider the person as "with" you, not "against" you.

3. *Focus on accepting the information and suggestions offered rather than on defending what you did.* Consider what is said as material for you to think about and weigh on your own at a later time. The nature of advice is such that you need only to hear it and not necessarily to act on it. Listen and even take notes so as to ensure your remembering and to indicate your sincerity of hearing what the feedback is. Even if there is some doubt on whether you will act on the advice given, say, "Thanks, I appreciate your suggestion. Give me some time to think this over." Do not say, "Yes, but . . . ," or "I've tried that before and it didn't work," or "You don't understand what really happened," or some other similar phrase indicating a rejection of the message being sent to you.

4. *Focus on improving rather than maintaining the status quo.* Keep in mind that the purpose of feedback is to offer you springboards for improvement. Make a resolution to try at least one new thing suggested by someone else or yourself based on the comments you receive. A positive approach will help you listen attentively and open-mindedly, so you can pick up that one new idea.

5. *Focus on seeking specific, concrete suggestions regarding your performance rather than abstractions about your approach or attitude.* Since you want to improve your discussion leadership, you need to improve what you *do* during the discussion. What you need to do and must do in order to improve is to perform in a better way. For this reason you need to seek com-

ments about what you did and what you *can do* in the future. Suggestions like "You should be warmer to the group" and "Be democratic" are not as helpful to you as "Sit closer to the group," "Ask the group to determine the next topic for discussion by consensus or even by vote—don't impose your topic on us," and "Summarize periodically, so we don't lose sight of what's been said already." Seek out concrete suggestions about *performance*.

6. *Focus on clarifying what's been said to you rather than passively absorbing a lecture from someone.* Ask the person to clarify the message to you so that you can easily follow it. Once the message is clear to you, you can begin to formulate possible avenues leading to improvement. Just because you are receiving feedback doesn't mean you are giving up your right to ask for clarity and specificity.

7. *Focus on understanding the sender's vantage point rather than on indicating your own vantage point.* If you can understand the vantage point of the sender, then you can better understand the perception of your behavior and the suggestions offered for improvement. For example, if you clearly understood that the person giving you feedback had the role of final recapitulator for the first time, then you can better cope with the suggestion to give specific instructions regarding what, when, and how to perform this role. There is little or no value in your indicating to the sender that you had almost no time before the discussion began to provide help to him or her.

8. *Focus on allowing the person to give you feedback in a personally comfortable way rather than in a structured way predetermined by you.* It may be difficult for a discussant to give you feedback, even though you specifically solicit it in a sincere way. The discussant may doubt your intentions or feel shaky about saying things to the leader of the discussion. For this reason you should focus on making the conditions comfortable for the discussant to give you feedback. You may have to sit with the discussant at his or her office, or desk, or seat, or in a lounge rather than at your desk, or seat, or on your "turf." You may find it better to talk at the drinking fountain or coffee urn, standing around in a casual way where the discussant feels comfortable. Allow the discussant to choose the conditions and time, if

necessary, so as to facilitate feedback. If you determine the conditions and time, the discussant may give you no feedback at all because she or he may consider this as unpleasant or uncomfortable.

9. *Check the feedback you receive from a discussant by summarizing the main points for both of you.* An excellent technique is to summarize the main ideas raised during your feedback conversation. You will have a good way to show that you understand the points raised according to the fundamental guidelines offered here for giving, soliciting, and receiving feedback. The act of summarizing will simultaneously serve as a device to remembering what you have received.

EVALUATING YOUR DISCUSSION LEADERSHIP

By the time you finish giving feedback to others, giving feedback to yourself, soliciting feedback, and receiving feedback, you will have an abundance of information about what happened during the discussion. This information is necessary for evaluating your discussion leadership. Although you do not need to evaluate yourself in order to improve, there is some temptation and inclination to evaluate in all of us.

If you do wish to evaluate your discussion leadership fully, then you will need to state explicitly what is already implicit in your self-rating, as done on the forms presented earlier. That is to say, you need to set down clearly and forthrightly what are for you the criteria of good discussion leadership. The selected criteria must be your own or at least your own personal weighing or rank ordering of someone else's criteria. In order to evaluate anything, you need criteria. To identify instances of good discussion leadership you need criteria to tell you what constitutes them. What is more you must put a weighing on the criteria. For example, two leaders may both value crystallizing and questioning highly but one may still value the skill of crystallizing more than questioning. The second leader may see questioning as the most important skill.

You can determine your own criteria by responding to some questions.

Guideline Questions for Evaluating a Discussion

1. What do I consider to be the qualities of good discussion leadership?
2. How important are these qualities?
3. What is the most important quality listed above?
4. What is the second most important quality? The third? The fourth? . . .

In answering these questions, you should draw on our previous sections concerning what is a discussion, discussion skills, how to plan a discussion, how to prevent and solve discussion problems, and the self-survey of discussion leadership. You may find that your criteria shift somewhat depending on the group, the time, the topic, and the location. For example, the key criterion with one group may be the amount of participation you are able to elicit; with another group discussing the very same topic, you may decide that the skill of contributing is the main element in your evaluation. For this reason no rigid set of criteria to suit all discussions at all times appears here.

Once you are clear about your criteria, you need to match criteria with information. That is, you must determine if there is evidence to show that your actions in this particular discussion met your criteria. Did you in this discussion question, contribute facts, explanations, and opinions, crystallize, verbally support the discussants, and prevent some problems from arising? If you did and your significant criteria involve these skills, then you need to decide to what degree you performed them. That is, did you perform these skills so well that you will label your discussion leadership as outstanding? Or, will you call your leadership average?

There is no way to adequately quantify the evaluation of discussion leadership so that you can know precisely whether or not you were outstanding, good, average, or poor. There is no precise procedure to offer here besides mentioning that you must gather information, decide on your own criteria, establish your own gradations on a scale from a high of outstanding to a low of poor, and then match all these factors together. There is no way that you can precisely measure all the subjective factors in a discussion.

This lack of exactitude exists because evaluation is subjective by nature, and there is no way to make it objective and precise. Even doing complicated statistical treatments of 1,000 questionnaires all giving their individual judgments of your discussion leadership on a seven-point scale from outstanding to poor will not avoid the subjective nature of evaluation. You may know that 78 percent of people believe your leadership to be outstanding and that the data are statistically significant at a .05 level of probability. But you still haven't avoided the subjective question of what constitutes outstanding discussion leadership and whether you yourself believe your discussion leadership to be outstanding for that specific discussion.

You will have some help in your evaluation procedure if you use the Post-Discussion Reaction form (page 118) mentioned earlier. The first question on the form requests the discussant to give an overall general rating of the discussion on a seven-point scale from outstanding to poor. If you use this form, it is advisable for you to fill out one personally *before* reading the completed ones so that you can have an uncolored way of comparing your own view with the other discussants.

In short, you don't need to rate your discussion leadership if you wish to improve because the feedback information is sufficient for your purposes. If you do decide to rate your discussion leadership, then you must match your information with the criteria you've established so you can arrive at a judgment. Of course, somewhere along the line you must decide how you will use the rating once you get it. What purpose will it serve? How will you benefit from it? What will you do with it once you have it?

8

IMPROVING DISCUSSION LEADERSHIP

THIS FINAL AND BRIEF CHAPTER TIES TOGETHER THE PREVIOUS ones by concentrating on improving discussion leadership. You can think or talk about leading a discussion and all it entails, but you need only one or two opportunities of leading one to come to the sober realization that discussion leadership is complex and demanding. Everyone, but everyone, who reflects on the discussions he or she has led begins to seriously seek ways to improve. No one is the perfect discussion leader who never needs to take steps for improvement.

Once you have thought about the nature of discussion and the nature of leadership, led a discussion or two, and then sought feedback along the lines suggested in Chapter 7, Discussion Feedback and Evaluation, you may have already begun walking on the path leading to improvement. To help you proceed more smoothly and systematically, you should complete the Improving Discussion Leadership form and retake the Self-Survey of Discussion Leadership.

COMPLETING THE IMPROVING DISCUSSION LEADERSHIP FORM

A major device for improving your discussion leadership is to complete the following form, Improving Discussion Leadership, each time you finish leading a discussion and begin reflecting on where and how to improve in the future. The structure of the form deserves your attention so that you can understand the approach toward improvement built into it.

Identify One Item of Concern

Note that the first item after the heading asks you to identify one element of particular concern to you. This concentration on one element—not two or three or four or more—is consistent with the guidelines on feedback stating that you should give, solicit, and receive only a manageable amount of feedback each time. Here you identify just one area you wish to work on at a time. You indeed may need to work on several areas as indicated by the feedback you have received. Nevertheless, you should concentrate on only one area at a time so that the task before you does not become overwhelming. If you try to work on several areas, you may well drown in things to do and thus render yourself unable to lead and improve.

Identify Future Actions

The next three sets of items go together to identify specific actions for you to do. These also are consistent with the guidelines on feedback. The top set asks you to specify three new things to try—new behaviors that can propel you forward. It says implicitly that there are always new alternatives and fresh ways to proceed.

Identify Things to Maintain/Increase

The middle set implicitly states that you have done some things well already and that you need to be aware of these so that you can keep up the good work. No discussion leader performs 100 percent poorly, and thus there are always some things to maintain or increase.

Improving Discussion Leadership

Discussion Leader _____

Discussion Title _____ Date: _____ Time: _____

Element of particular concern: _____

Some New Things to Try:

   A.

   B.

   C.

Some Things to Maintain/Increase:

   A.

   B.

   C.

Some Things to Stop/Reduce/Avoid:

   A.

   B.

   C.

Date of next discussion? _____

Material to read and think about? _____

Who will give feedback next time? _____

Things to Stop/Reduce/Avoid

The last set of items, on the other hand, recognizes that no discussion leader is totally perfect, and thus there are always some things that should be stopped or reduced or avoided in the future.

The three sets of items together present a positive approach to improvement. Too often people seek to improve by identifying negative behaviors. But, although necessary, stopping poor behavior is not sufficient. Telling yourself what *not* to do is not at all the same as telling yourself what *to do*. When you are leading a discussion you need to know what to do—leading is doing, leading is active. To fulfill this need of knowing what to do, you have two positive sets of items. Hence, you have a positive approach to improvement rather than a negative one.

To further appreciate the reasoning behind the combining of three sets of items to yield an effective, positive approach, consider how we learn any concept. Take the concept of a "gleep." Your friend identifies six items and each time she says, "This is not a gleep." After six times you know what *isn't* a gleep but you don't know what *is* a gleep. Even after ten times you do not know what a gleep is. Only when your friend points to an item and says, "This is a gleep," do you know what a gleep is. Now you can differentiate a gleep from a non-gleep. You may still be a bit shaky, but you've come a long way toward having a clear concept of a gleep. You need a positive instance to help you, even though you have many negative instances.

However, do not dismiss the value of a negative instance of a gleep. Consider now that your friend begins in the opposite way. If she points to six items and each time she says, "This is a gleep," you have an idea of what a gleep is, but even after ten items you may be unsure. When she finally points to one and says, "This is not a gleep," you have come a long way and have a more solid hold on the concept. Now you definitely can differentiate a gleep from a non-gleep. You need a negative instance to help you even though you have some positive instances. You need both positive and negative instances, but you need an emphasis on the positive so you can know what a gleep is.

Similarly, you need to concentrate on what you need to do positively in order to improve as a discussion leader rather than on what you ought not to do. Listing all and only the negative things in your behavior will not direct you to specific positive items for you to do. Nor will listing only positive items tell you what to avoid. It is on this basis that the three sets of items on Improving Discussion Leadership form combine to help you improve your leadership behavior by emphasizing the positive while giving some recognition to the negative.

The bottom set of three questions are meant to be spurs to your attempts and preparation. The first question asks you to specify the date of your next discussion, giving you the encouragement to lead another discussion. The second question asks you to specify what you can read or think about that will help you prepare by getting you in the right frame of mind. The third question asks you to specify the person who can and will offer you feedback. The implicit statement here is that you will lead another discussion and start the entire reflective process all over again. You will use that feedback to reflect on your next discussion and also to plan the one after next for such is the function of feedback.

The completing of the Improving Discussion Leadership form will be a benefit to you because it will require you to move from looking at what you have already done to what you can do in the future. It is a thin line between reflecting on the past and planning for the future. You are never sure exactly when you cross that line, but the important point is that you indeed do cross it. This form will guide you across it and put you safely on the path of improvement.

RETAKING THE SELF-SURVEY OF DISCUSSION LEADERSHIP

To see how you have changed at least in your perceptions of your discussion leadership behavior since you began reading this book you should respond again to the Self-Survey of Discussion Leadership at the end of this chapter. Do *not* check back to your first set of responses or refer to your scoring sheet yet. Respond to each item in a fresh way, score yourself, and then compare your two sets of responses yielding your two Discussion Leadership Scores. Go through each of the 50 items carefully to note differences in your responses from then till now. This process will further sensitize you to the areas in which you need improvement.

Many people play piano today, and some are outstanding pianists by virtue of their talent and practice. Some pianists play poorly. All piano players can improve with good guidance. So it is with discussion leadership. Many people lead discussions, and some are outstanding leaders. Some lead discussions poorly. As with pianists, every discussion leader can improve with good guidance. By conscientiously following the ideas presented in this book you can surely improve as a discussion leader. You need not sit back—you can lead. And you can be an excellent discussion leader.

Self-Survey of Discussion Leadership

Circle the appropriate letter next to each item to indicate your response.

A= Always	O= Occasionally	N= Never
F= Frequently	S= Seldom	

In a discussion group I —

A F O S N   1. accept negative behavior of individuals as everyone's problem, not just of the individuals who are disruptive.

A F O S N   2. am aware of the verbal tones I use and the messages they convey.

A F O S N   3. arrange for a physical environment that fosters positive exchanges among the discussants.

A F O S N   4. ask others about the relevancy of their remarks.

A F O S N   5. ask questions of others to elicit needed data, explanations, or opinions.

A F O S N   6. ask the discussants to draw conclusions as we end the discussion.

A F O S N   7. boast, horse around, or talk sarcastically.

A F O S N   8. change the topic and cause the group to leave its task temporarily.

A F O S N   9. check my perceptions about what's going on by asking questions such as "Am I right in saying that you feel that . . .?"

A F O S N 10. clarify points made by others, clearing up misunderstandings, definitions, or explanations.

A F O S N 11. consider leadership of the discussion as the responsibility of everyone.

A F O S N 12. contribute to the formulation of the group's goals and procedures.

A F O S N 13. dominate the discussion.

A F O S N 14. encourage and allow the discussion questions to be answered by all the discussants, especially the quiet and shy ones.

A F O S N 15. focus the discussion at various points so that the group knows what the specific topic is and does not drift.

A F O S N 16. force quiet discussants to participate.

A F O S N 17. interfere with the group's task by arguing, bringing up "dead issues," or persistently pleading a special interest position.

A F O S N 18. interrupt other speakers to say what's on my mind and relevant at the moment.

A F O S N 19. keep track of time and keep the discussion on schedule.

A F O S N 20. let others know when I've modified a position I took earlier.

A F O S N 21. listen attentively to others.

A F O S N 22. listen only to experts on the topic under discussion.

A F O S N 23. offer compromises when the group is dead-locked during a controversial issue.

A F O S N 24. offer needed facts and explanations to help the discussion.

A F O S N 25. praise others when they make pertinent re-marks.

A F O S N 26. prepare a concise introduction of the topic to make it clear what we're discussing.

A F O S N 27. prepare a discussion strategy based on the major questions that need to be answered.

A F O S N 28. prepare an outline of the topic with suggested time limits for each phase of the discussion.

A F O S N 29. probe others for further points for clarifica-tion.

A F O S N 30. propose future activities as follow-ups to the discussion.

A F O S N 31. offer my opinions and justifications to help the discussion.

A F O S N 32. provide for a written record of the high points of the discussion.

A F O S N 33. raise the question of how the group should proceed in conducting the discussion.

A F O S N 34. reflect back to the group the verbal and non-verbal messages I receive from other dis-cussants.

A F O S N 35. speak briefly so that others have the opportu-nity to talk.

A F O S N 36. state the essence of the discussion at various points as we proceed.

A F O S N 37. suggest alternative ways to view a point al-ready raised.

A F O S N 38. suggest special discussion roles for various people as a way of involving and supporting them.

A F O S N 39. suggest ways to solve problems that have arisen because of tension and conflict in the group.

A F O S N   40. suggest when and how the group can deal with peripheral issues not taken up at the moment.

A F O S N   41. support the right of others to speak, especially those with unpopular points of view.

A F O S N   42. take steps, even before the discussion begins, to break up potentially harmful cliques.

A F O S N   43. threaten others with the pointed questions I ask and the tone in which I ask them.

A F O S N   44. try to prevent problems and a negative climate from arising.

A F O S N   45. try to reduce tension with humor or friendly comments so as to reconcile disagreements among people.

A F O S N   46. use analogies to help clarify the meaning of what has been said.

A F O S N   47. use guests as speakers and resource people.

A F O S N   48. use my physical location and posture to convey a positive nonverbal message.

A F O S N   49. view discussion as a game with winners and losers.

A F O S N   50. withdraw from the discussion and show signs of being noninvolved or indifferent.

Scoring Sheet for Self-Survey of Discussion Leadership

Write your score next to the number for each item in the self-survey.

For Columns I, II, III, and IV		For Column V	
Always	= A = 4	Never	= N = 4
Frequently	= F = 3	Seldom	= S = 3
Occasionally	= O = 2	Occasionally	= O = 2
Seldom	= S = 1	Frequently	= F = 1
Never	= N = 0	Always	= A = 0

I	II	III	IV	V
1 ____	14 ____	28 ____	38 ____	7 ____
2 ____	15 ____	29 ____	39 ____	8 ____
3 ____	19 ____	30 ____	40 ____	13 ____
4 ____	20 ____	31 ____	41 ____	16 ____

5 _____ 21 _____ 32 _____ 42 _____ 17 _____

6 _____ 23 _____ 33 _____ 44 _____ 18 _____

9 _____ 24 _____ 34 _____ 45 _____ 22 _____

10 _____ 25 _____ 35 _____ 46 _____ 43 _____

11 _____ 26 _____ 36 _____ 47 _____ 49 _____

12 _____ 27 _____ 37 _____ 48 _____ 50 _____

Total _____ Total _____ Total _____ Total _____ Total _____

Total Column I _____
Total Column II _____
Total Column III _____
Total Column IV _____
Total Column V _____

Put your total Discussion Leadership Score here: ☐ The maximum is 200 points.

APPENDIX
Mini-Course in Logic for the Discussion Leader

As you lead a discussion you must concern yourself simultaneously with the two elements of content and discussion process. In addition to these, there is a third element of a discussion you must be alert to as the discussion progresses. This is the logic of the discussion, which deals with whether what is said is valid or fallacious. Some people consider the element of logic as part of content while others consider it as part of process. No matter how you personally want to label and classify logic, you must keep your eye on it as leader of the discussion. It is important because it is connected to what is said and to whom, when, and how what is said is said. If you pay attention to the logic of a discussion, you can save many a discussion from ending in a disaster and help many more succeed by staying on the right track.

Below are some basic considerations for you to keep in mind.* They do not constitute a course in logic or a synopsis of a college philosophy course entitled Logic 101. Their purpose is to give you some help in dealing with issues that arise in *every* discussion.

---

*I am indebted to John Passmore, *Talking Things Over,* third edition (Melbourne: Melbourne University Press, 1963) for directing my attention to these matters in leading a discussion. I draw on Chapters 5 and 6 of Passmore's brief booklet in the first three sections of this mini-course.

MATTERS SUPPORTED BY REFERRING TO AN AUTHORITY

Often discussants will support what they say be referring to an authority on the topic. For example, "The earth was formed by a huge explosion—a big bang—18 million years ago, according to Professor Simon." To keep the discussion straight you can test the support for the statement by asking yourself at least four questions:

1. Is this a matter on which expert knowledge or opinion is decisive?
2. Is the person referred to really an authority on this matter?
3. Has the discussant quoted the authority correctly?
4. Is the quotation (or paraphrase of it) pertinent at this point in the discussion?

RULES OF ARGUMENT

When discussants compare items or try to show a causal relation between them, it is helpful to keep in mind six common rules of argument.

1. Just because two things have one characteristic in common, you may not validly draw any further conclusions about their relationship.
2. Just because two things are different from one another in one or several respects, you may not validly conclude that a characteristic that one has doesn't also belong to the other.
3. Just because two things are different from a third thing, you may not validly conclude anything about their relationship to each other.
4. Just because you find two things together at one point in time, you may not validly conclude that you will always find them together.
5. Just because one thing precedes another, you may not validly conclude that the first thing causes the second one.

6. Just because one thing always follows another thing, you may not validly conclude that whenever you find the second one the first must have preceded it.

PSYCHOLOGICAL DEVICES USED IN ARGUMENTS

In addition to knowing rules of argument, it is helpful to recognize that there are some psychological devices that can be used to convince people about particular ideas. These psychological devices involve transferring one idea to another.

Labeling

You get others to disapprove (or approve) of something by labelling it unfavorably (or favorably). For example, "This idea is no good—it's just the same old terrorist idea with a new name."

Abusing or Praising the Person

You get others to disapprove (or approve) of something by commenting on the person connected with the issues rather than on the issue itself. For example, "I agree that nuclear energy will be good for our area. David Brown, a guy who has the best sense of humor in this whole town, was talking to me about it just yesterday. If he likes it with is keen sense of humor, it's got to be right for us."

Inconsistency

You get others to disapprove of something by pointing out the inconsistency of people connected with the item or idea. You talk about this inconsistency and not the issue itself. For example, "How can you believe the doctors when they tell you that cigarettes cause cancer? Why? Doctors are known as heavy smokers themselves. If cigarettes cause cancer, the doctors wouldn't smoke them."

Appeal to Motives

You get others to disapprove of something by showing that the people who support it have personal gain in mind. You talk about motives and not the issue itself. For example, "I don't think we should support the interstate highway program. After all, look who's supporting it, the truckers and the civil engineers society and we know that they're just trying to keep their jobs."

Sarcasm

You get others to disapprove of something by dealing sarcastically with the person or issue associated with it. If the person associated with the issue becomes angry because of sarcasm, all the better because angry people make errors in their thinking and easily lose in disputation. For example, "It's no wonder you're leaning toward supporting this issue. You're confused as you usually are. If you'll restate the issue in simple terms without all those inane anecdotes, even you'll see the the solution offered is worthless."

Analogy

You get others to disapprove (or approve) of something by using an unfavorable (or favorable) analogy. This device works because on the spur of the moment it is difficult to figure just where the analogy breaks down and doesn't hold. For example, "We ought to support the U.S. Olympics Committee and their efforts to train athletes. It's like when you were in college and you were supposed to support the college basketball team and cheer for them at their games."

VALID AND INVALID FORMS OF CONDITIONAL REASONING

When people talk in terms of "If this is X, then Y is the case," they are using conditional reasoning as signaled by the "If . . . , then . . ." language. There are four basic forms of conditional reasoning. Below are brief examples of each of the four with a notation of whether that type is valid or invalid reasoning. Each starts with a *conditional premise* containing an *antecedent* and a *consequent*. Next comes a *second premise* affirming or denying one part of the conditional premise. Then comes a *conclusion*.

Type 1: Affirming the Antecedent (Valid reasoning)

Conditional Prem.:	If Miami is in Florida, then Miami is in the United States
2nd Prem.:	Miami is in Florida
Conclusion:	Miami is in the United States (Valid)

Type 2: Affirming the Consequent (Invalid reasoning)

Conditional Prem.:	If Miami is in Florida, then Miami is in the United States
2nd Prem.:	Miami is in the United States
Conclusion:	Miami is in Florida (Invalid)

Type 3: Denying the Antecedent (Invalid reasoning)

Conditional Prem.:	If Miami is in Florida, then Miami is in the United States
2nd Prem.:	Miami is not in Florida
Conclusion:	Miami is not in the United States (Invalid)

Type 4: Denying the Consequent (Valid reasoning)

Conditional Prem.:	If Miami is in Florida, then Miami is in the United States
2nd Prem.:	Miami is not in the United States
Conclusion:	Miami is not in Florida (Valid)

FALLACIES[†]

The following brief but comprehensive selection on fallacies comes from a handbook on critical reasoning, embodying an approach to reasoning skills developed by Professor Clyde Evans of the Department of Philosophy, University of Massa-

---

[†]Reprinted from *Critical Thinking and Reasoning* (Albany, New York: The University of the State of New York, The Board of Regents, 1976) pp. 64–68.

chusetts at Boston. The ability to recognize fallacies as they occur is helpful to the progress and eventual success of the discussion.

Relatively few ways exist in which persons can reason or argue correctly, but a host of ways in which they can do so incorrectly. An error or mistake in reasoning is a fallacy, and the reasoning itself, in that case, fallacious. Recall the fallacies of denying the antecedent and affirming the consequent discussed regarding conditional arguments. These were formal fallacies; that is, the errors committed were errors because of the form of the argument. Also, with regard to syllogisms, rules can be formulated which indicate that certain kinds of syllogisms are always erroneous and thus fallacious, again because of the form.

Some fallacies are committed not because of the form of the argument, but specifically because of the content. Isolating several different types of reasoning or argumentation which, because of the nature of what is said, are illegitimate or fallacious in the particular moves they make, can prove fruitful. Only a few of the more prominent types will be listed. Sometimes, these types overlap. Also, the names given here may differ from those given to the same fallacy by other writers. It may prove helpful to keep the following classifications in mind:

fallacy: an erroneous piece of reasoning;

formal fallacy: a fallacy which occurs because of an error in the form of the argument, independent of its content;

informal fallacy: a fallacy which occurs specifically because of the content of the argument.

1. The Ad Hominem Fallacy—This fallacy derives its name from the Latin expression "ad hominem," meaning "[directed] to the man." The fallacy consists in attacking the person rather than the person's argument. The basic form of this fallacy is:

   Person P makes statement Z
   P is a "bad guy"
   Z is false (bad, wrong, undesirable, etc.)

   Ex. "Principal Carter proposed this grievance procedure for teachers. But he didn't even get his contract renewed for next year. Who's going to listen to anything he says?" This is fallacious because clearly the merits of the proposed grievance procedure are completely independent from whether Principal Carter was re-hired or not (which, of course, is not necessarily correlated with his competency as a principal).

2. Two Wrongs Make a Right—This fallacy says essentially: "If they can get away with it, then so can I."

   Ex. It is all right for the U.S. to sell military arms to all the countries in the Middle East, even though the same arms are then used to conduct war against each other, because the Soviet Union does it, too.

3. Common Practice or Appeal to Popularity—The basic form of this fallacy is:

   It is commonly done (or done by the majority).
   It is right (good, desirable, excusable) for us to do it.

   Ex. Justification of huge salary increase for policemen on the grounds that firemen, sanitation workers, transit workers, etc., all received large increases.

4. Straw Man—This fallacy consists in attacking a position which sounds like your opponent's position but which is really different. Here, one deliberately poses a weak and vulnerable position (the straw man) which, when it is destroyed, will hopefully cast doubt on the position of the opponent.

   Ex. Al Capp quotes Mayor John Lindsay as saying: "The Americans I have unending admiration for are the guys who say, 'I simply will not serve in the Army of the United States and I am willing to take the consequences. Those are the guys who are heroic.'" Capp then remarks: "And so, if Lindsay is elected, his first act as commander-in-chief will, no doubt, be to withdraw the Army from everywhere . . ."

5. False Dilemma—The reduction of alternatives or possibilities to only two when, in fact, there are others. Usually these two are constructed in such a way that one alternative is so "horrible" that no one in his right mind would choose it. This leaves only the other alternative, which just happens to be the one espoused by the speaker in the first place.

   Ex. Either you stamp down with force on this student unrest now or all learning will grind to a halt at this university.

6. Begging the Question—Failure to give any support to the very

issue in question, usually by assuming in the premises that which one purports to prove in the conclusion.

Ex. Judith Crist is not a competent film critic because she is prejudiced; she is prejudiced because she does not like films with a lot of sex and violence; she does not like films with a lot of sex and violence because she is not a competent film critic.

7. Appeal to Authority—This fallacy says: "Person P says it, and P is an authority, thus whatever she or he espouses must be true or good." This is fallacious when it appeals to an improper authority.

Ex. Joe Namath is shown advertising panty hose. It would be perfectly legitimate to consult Joe as an authority in football. But we have no reason to believe that he is an authority on panty hose. Thus, an appeal to him as an authority is improper.

8. Appeal to Tradition—This fallacy says, "We should do it this way or think this way just because it's always been this way."

Ex. Teachers should penalize and/or punish students for not having their work done on time because it has always been this way.

9. Irrelevant Reason—Use of considerations totally irrelevant to the conclusion or to the issue.

Ex. Vote for Sidney Brown. He's a veteran.

10. Slippery Slope/Domino Theory—This is the fallacious assumption that the first step in a possible series of steps inevitably leads to the rest. This is the familiar "once you open the flood gates . . ." argument.

Ex. If you let her stay out past 10:00 p.m., the first thing you know she'll be out all night.

(This might also be considered an instance of the straw man fallacy.)

A common variation of this fallacy is the domino theory, the conclusion that if A falls, so will B, C, etc.

Ex. If South Vietnam goes Communist, so will Laos, Cambodia, Thailand and all of Indo-China, and the Far East.

11. Jumping to Conclusion—Basing a conclusion on relevant but insufficient evidence (closely connected to fallacy of Hasty Generalization).

> Ex. A news story reporting a local flurry of flag-stealing quoted one citizen as saying: "They took both the flag and the pole. This just thoroughly demonstrates the lack of law and order in our society today."

12. Argument from Analogy—This is the fallacious assumption that just because two things have several characteristics in common, they will have yet another. The basic form of the fallacy:

> X has characteristics a, b, c, d, e
> Y has characteristics a, b, c, d, e
> *X also has characteristic f*
> Y also has characteristic f

> Ex. Sidney, who is Jewish, has been married twice before to Catholic women; and neither marriage worked out. He should know better than to get mixed-up with this new Catholic woman. It'll never work.

13. Distraction—Turning the direction of an argument away from the point at issue by means of an emotive device or irrelevant consideration.

> Ex. On the television program "Sanford and Son," Fred Sanford is defending himself in court on a traffic violation. He begins to cross-examine the arresting officer by asking, "What do you have against black drivers?"

14. Equivocation—Changing the sense or meaning of a word or phrase in a way which makes the argument sound more persuasive than it really is.

> Ex. Any country which holds elections is a democracy.
> *The Soviet Union holds elections.*
> Therefore, the Soviet Union is a democracy.

> The expression "holds elections" clearly means two different things in the two premises.

15. Inconsistency—Saying something now which is logically incompatible with what one said at another time; i.e., contradicting oneself. A special version of inconsistency consists in apply-

ing certain standards or principles to someone else, but failing to apply them to oneself.

Ex. Richard Nixon, September 13, 1966: "He [President Johnson] owes it to the people to come clean and tell them exactly what the plans are: the people should be told now, and not after the elections." Richard Nixon, March 10, 1968, now a candidate for president: "No one with this responsibility who is seeking office should give away any of his bargaining position in advance . . . under no circumstances should a man say what he would do next January."

16. Oversimplification—Leaving out relevant considerations in an attempt to make issue appear simpler than it is.

17. Slanting—A form of misrepresentation by means of suggesting something which is not true.

Ex. I notice that Ms. Cedarleaf sometimes stays after school with her pupils. At least somebody in this place cares about students.

18. Cliché Fallacy—Unsupported claim that something is a concrete instance of the general principle contained in a familiar proverb or aphorism. The use of a cliché is not in itself fallacious. It is the failure to show either that (1) the general maxim itself is reliable or (2) this is indeed one of the instances covered by the general maxim.

Ex. Several people trying to prepare dinner and getting in each other's way. "Too many cooks spoil the broth."

19. Appeal to Pity—Attempt to win assent by appealing to pity and sympathy of the listener.

Ex. "Mr. Gallus, if you don't give me a B on this exam, I won't pass this course, and then I won't be able to graduate on time, and I already have this job waiting for me."

20. Complex Question—Asking a question which assumes something which the person questioned regards as false.

Ex. "Have you stopped beating your wife?"

Index